"This book will challenge, but it will also ( sibility that walking with the Lord Jesus through the presence of the Holy Spirit

Former U.S. Director,

"Roc Bottomly's journey and understanding of the vital blend of God's Word and God's Spirit will inspire each of us who long to know and serve Jesus Christ with all our heart, mind, and strength."
- Paul Stanley
Former International Vice President of The Navigators,
Co-author of *Connecting*

"Roc Bottomly has been learning how to build bridges from the Word to the Spirit for twenty-five years, and he knows what the body of Christ can experience when we are unified and not concerned with labels. *More!* is a practical guide to understanding how God is uniting His family."
- Kent Humphreys
Author of *Show and Tell* and *Lasting Investments*

"Anyone who is honestly seeking to see how the Father's Word and the Holy Spirit's work coexist and complement each other will be enthralled by this spiritual page-turner. Roc's love of God's Word has led him to honestly view the Holy Spirit's work in a way that is much needed and clearly shared in this hallmark work."
- Tom Phillips
Author of *Revival Signs* and *Ignite Your Passion for God*

"At last! A book that practically and biblically shows believers how they can know the piercing power that comes when the Word and the Spirit flow together. Bravo, Roc, for your candor and for the challenge to press forward until we personally experience the promised power."
- Lorraine Pintus
Co-author of *Intimate Issues* and *Gift-Wrapped by God*

"*More!* is a delightfully engaging companion for a journey of discovery that is as wondrous as it is perilous."
-Ken Gire
Author of *Windows of the Soul* and *Moments with the Savior*

MORE!

MORE!

Encouraging those who love the Bible to experience the promised power of the Spirit

ROC BOTTOMLY

Trilogy Christian Publishers A Wholly Owned Subsidiary of Trinity Broadcasting Network
2442 Michelle Drive Tustin, CA 92780

Rights Department, 2442 Michelle Drive, Tustin, CA 92780.

Trilogy Christian Publishing/ TBN and colophon are trademarks of Trinity Broadcasting Network.

For information about special discounts for bulk purchases, please contact Trilogy Christian Publishing.

Trilogy Disclaimer: The views and content expressed in this book are those of the author and may not necessarily reflect the views and doctrine of Trilogy Christian Publishing or the Trinity Broadcasting Network.

Manufactured in the United States of America

10 9 8 7 6 5 4 3 2 1

Library of Congress Cataloging-in-Publication Data is available.

ISBN: 978-1-64088-585-1

E-ISBN: 978-1-64088-586-8

DEDICATION

New wine must be poured into new wineskins. And no one after drinking old wine wants the new, for he says, 'The old is better."

Luke 5:38-39

To   John and Jan Bingaman — consummate "new wineskins." You have tasted the old and the new and have never said, "The old is better."

Thanks for being my periscope into the strange and wonderful world of the Spirit church.

Thanks for modeling truth and power with such grace and maturity. Thanks for enduring the birth pangs of continuous renewal.

There is a friend who sticks closer than a brother.

Proverbs 18:24

Contents

STUDY GUIDE CONTENTS

For each of the twelve chapters, there is an opportunity for "Searching the Scriptures" in the often-unexplored area of the Holy Spirit. As you work through this study, you will look at many of the important passages in both the Old and New Testaments that teach us about the Spirit — who He is and how He helps.

ACKNOWLEDGEMENTS

Like so many books, this one had a long gestation period. In this case, it was twenty-four years. And like many other books, the "knitting together in the womb" involved a lot of people, most of whom have no idea how formative they were.

John and Jan Bingaman: You've been telling me how to pour new wine into old wineskins from the beginning. Our first conversation started with John saying, "Now, Roc, we know you are new here (I'd been pastor at Covenant Community Church for about 10 days), and we'd like to suggest a few changes that would make things a lot better." And so it's been for the past twenty-four years! Best friends. Fellow laborers. Co-pastors. Obsessive seekers of God. Willing to learn and do anything that might give a clearer view of the Father, Son, or Holy Spirit — at absolutely any cost. And what a high price you have paid. Giant thanks. I'd never have gone beyond talking about the possibilities without you.

The people and elders at Covenant Community Church: You were my first congregation and for ten years absorbed all the mistakes of my rookie ministry. When it comes to loving one another, you do it better than any I've seen. Thanks for enduring my first awkward steps in the things of the Spirit and loving me anyway. Special thanks to Jack and Jodie Hough. Your lives of prayer and listening to the Spirit taught Bev and me early on that God is very near.

The people and elders at Pulpit Rock Church: Thanks for giving me the courage to try new things — a conference on spiritual warfare (before it was considered "safe"); new music and freedom in worship (always high risk); healing prayer teams in the worship services (radical at the time); a listening prayer ministry (did we really allow this?); elders anointing with oil and praying for the sick (at a respected Bible church). You opened the door for God to work as far and as fast as He could without ripping the communal fabric. Thanks for opening the gates — and, when needed, applying the brakes. Thanks to Joanie Thompson, who persevered in listening for the Spirit's voice and using His healing power before we had the vocabulary to make it respectable. Special thanks to Steve and Bonnie Aldrich, whose years on the mission field and personal encounters with God gave us permission to expect more from Him than we'd seen before. What a great church!

The people and elders at Bridgeway Church: What incredibly happy and courageous pioneers! Do you people have no fear? How rare to combine passionate devotion and bold exploration in one religious body. But you have done it and in the process provided far more than a book. You have provided a community that is doing this stuff. You have given all a place to visit to see a Word-Spirit church in action. Special thanks to "The Group" of high school and college students (all 25 years older and most married with kids and a hefty mortgage), who provided the zeal, energy, and push to birth Bridgeway: Al and Melissa King, Justin and Tiffany Fuller, Steve and Becky Hartman, and the rest of you who packed into the Bingaman's basement to worship and experience God's surprising presence. Thanks to Tom and Pam Ball, David and Myrna Lightfoot, Robert and Becky Gilbert, John and Kathy Phillips, Kathleen Blue, Kay Zahasky, and so many others who risked friendships and respectability to help give adult leadership to this highly suspect venture. Thanks to Charlie Hall, Brad Kilman, and Nathan and Christie Nockles, who led worship with such magnetic heart and skill. Let's face it: Most came in the early days of Bridgeway for your music and the hope it gave that God would come and do what He promised in His Book.

Finally, thanks to my precious wife, who believed enough in the message of this book to pay the high price of many unwanted times alone to see it finished. Pooh, we're done, and I'm coming home!

PREFACE

Let the word of Christ dwell in you richly.

Colossians 3:16

Be filled with the Spirit.

Ephesians 5:18

About What's Going On

Something wonderful is happening. There is a happy reunion in progress. It's a family reunion among those who love God. It's a reunion of those who have faithfully loved God's truth with those that have faithfully embraced his power. It's a reunion of Word and Spirit. And for all involved, there is great reason to celebrate as they embrace newfound family and discover missing pieces of life with God that have long been hidden among those on "the other side."

About You

Considering that you've picked up this book, you are probably already part of this reunion. And you are not alone. The latest research reports that in recent, more than fifty million believers have become part of "the mainstream church renewal,"[1] the technical term for what happens when evangelicals personally experience the promised power of the Holy Spirit— the power they have seen so clearly in the Bible they have faithfully read for years.

Chances are that you are personally experiencing a paradigm shift in the area of the promised power of the Spirit. Something unsettling has happened in your life — or in the life of your husband, wife, friend, or pastor.

You (or they) are probably somewhere in the process of discovering that God has provided us with *two* supernatural resources of staggering value: His Word *and* His Spirit. Of course, you have loved the Bible and the Holy Spirit for as long as you have followed God, but you are awakening to the possibility that there is a lot more to one of these — either Word or Spirit — than you ever imagined.

You may be a "Word" person who is discovering new ministries of the Spirit, or you may be a "Spirit" person who is discovering the new life that comes from understanding and living the Bible. You have somehow wandered through a gap in the wall that has for decades separated God-loving people into two neighborhoods: those who know the Bible and those who know the Spirit. Somehow you have met someone or heard or experienced something from the other side. If that's true, you are probably feeling amazed, confused, frightened, and excited. You may be unsure what to think, how to feel, who to tell, or what to do.

If this is you, intended or not and like it or not, you are part of a reunion arranged at the Highest Level. You are part of the reunion of Word and Spirit.

And this book is for you.

About Me

Since 1990, I have lived in the midst of this reunion. I stumbled into it quite by accident. It began for me with an exposure to intimate worship. Worship stirred an all-my-heart desire for God. New passion for God led to new compassion for people. Compassion for people led to a longing for the power to help them. The longing for power led to the Spirit, then to people who knew the Spirit, back to the Word to find out what the Spirit does and how to allow Him to do it in and through me, and finally back to real life to see what really works. And so it's gone for me.

In the course of all of this, I have pastored four churches through the Word-Spirit union with results ranging from dismal failure to significant progress. I know firsthand that the process stretches people to the limits. It has stretched me intellectually. I'm an engineer by training, unfamiliar and uncomfortable with the mysterious. It has stretched me emotionally. Passion and affection scare me. It has stretched me relationally. I've gained and lost friends in the process. It has stretched me theologically. Hearing His voice, feeling His presence, performing healing prayer, believing in angels and demons — my initial reaction was, *You've got to be kidding!* I have struggled to understand, believe, explain, sell, and keep the peace — in the church, in my family, and in my own soul. Yet after twenty-five years of watching this Word-Spirit union transform lives, I am left with the conclusion that the benefits far outweigh the strains and that God Himself is behind this happy reunion. God Himself is restoring the power of the Spirit to those who for a variety of reasons have lost it along the way but are willing to receive it.

About This Book

This book is designed to be read with Bible in hand and preferably with a like-hearted friend or group of friends. The Promised Power refers to the power of the Holy Spirit promised in the Scriptures. The best way to see these promises yourself is to search the Scriptures on your own.

To help you with this process, there is a study guide in the back of the book that provides a thorough Bible study of the person and work of the Holy Spirit (see the "Searching the Scriptures" section in the study guide that corresponds to each chapter in the book). To help you talk through what you are seeing in the Bible and experiencing in your life, the study guide also contains a "Sharing Your Life" section for each chapter of the book. These questions are excellent for guiding discussion with a friend or small group of fellow explorers.

Because the person and ministry of the Holy Spirit may represent both mysterious and unexplored territory, it is vital that you take the time to study the Scriptures for yourself. Your firsthand study will give you the firm convictions you'll need to make life changes. Companions in the process will provide needed balance and confidence.

An Invitation

If you are experiencing the union of Word and Spirit — if God is adding the mysterious working of the Spirit to your heritage in the Bible, or if He's adding the treasure of Scripture to your experience with the Spirit — this book should be helpful to you. It is not a technical defense of either the inspiration of Scripture or the power of the Spirit. Others have provided outstanding scholarly support for both of these from biblical, theological, and historical perspectives. My purpose is to provide a pastor's perspective. As one who has experienced the life-breathing effects of the Word-Spirit union in my own life, I want to:

- *celebrate* what God is doing in your life.

- *affirm* that you are on the right track in pursuing the benefits of both Word and Spirit to the full limits promised in the Scriptures.

- *encourage* you to continue to learn from the other side.

- *guide* you with some practical direction to keep your exploring responsible and fruitful.

Welcome to the union of Word and Spirit. It is not the panacea to all the pain of life. It will not answer all the questions, end all the groaning, heal all the diseases, or shield from all the injustices. These will come with the final union of the Groom and His bride. But this present union will provide fresh intimacy, zeal, and progress to all who join in.

So for all who have started down the Word-Spirit path, *read on and keep coming!*

PREFACE TO THE THIRD EDITION

This is the third edition of this book. In the fourteen years since the first edition, things have changed.

For the Church corporately, many more churches and individuals are embracing a life with God that expects more of the experience and power promised in the Scriptures. New leaders like Matt Chandler (Village Church, Dallas), Sam Storms (Bridgeway Church, Oklahoma City), Jimmy Seibert (Antioch Church, Waco), and Francis Chan (We Are Church, San Francisco) have been calling Bible-loving evangelicals to a far more robust life in the Spirit. Emerging movements like Acts 29, YWAM, Antioch Ministries International, Hillsong International, and Bethel Ministries – though different in specifics and still working out the details of doctrine and practice - are together providing training, worship, leadership and ministry experience to expose and equip thousands for a more biblically empowered life with Jesus. The fruit of these leaders, churches and movements is a new generation of impassioned disciples devoted to magnifying God's glory in their worship, fulfilling the Great Commission, and bringing the peace of the Kingdom to their worlds.

In short, in the last fourteen years the circle of those pursuing and experiencing the promised power of the Holy Spirit has grown significantly larger, and the impact has been fresh zeal for the next generation.

This is wonderful!

For me personally, two changes are unmistakable. First, my convictions about the wonder and import of both Word and Spirit have deepened.

Second, my desire to see all put the two together and walk on both spiritual legs has increased.

- Regarding the Bible... I have continued to read, study, memorize and live by the words of Scripture; and I have found now – some 50+ years down the road with God – that His Word is as essential to my well-being as at the beginning. The self-evident truth of the Bible strengthens my faith. The promises give peace to my naturally anxious heart. The messages about the future give hope to my aging body. The commands keep me from self-destruction. I love the Bible more than ever!

- Regarding the Spirit... The supernatural bursts of Spirit power that were novel, strange and sporadic fourteen years ago have become more familiar and regular. They are still wondrous, happy, and (I'm embarrassed to say) surprising; but they feel more normal. There is still fear... What will people think? Is what I'm "hearing" just me? What if God doesn't heal? There is still mystery... Why do only some get healed, delivered, and physically touched? Why does God speak to me about others but less often to me about me? Why do so many speak in tongues and so few interpret? There is still puzzling... Just how much of the authority of Jesus and His Apostles really extends to all? How do we clearly describe what we can realistically expect? But, this said, I have seen that where His People pray for the sick, listen for His voice, speak with authority to evil spirits, ask for spiritual gifts, and make space for God to work... well, wonderful things happen just like we read in The Book. Sure it is, "Sometimes He does and sometimes He doesn't"... but sometimes He *does!* And when He does, as in The Book, there is "great joy in that city." (Acts 8:8)

On a very personal note, Bev and I have seen our four children all flourish in their faith through the ups and downs of these past fourteen years. And they have all experienced significant ups and downs.

As we look back, we realized that as a family we made the shift into a Word-Spirit community just as they were entering their spiritually formative teen years. As a result, at just the point they were seriously making faith their own they got to experience the benefits of both hearing truth and seeing power. They got great instruction from church and school, and at the same time they experienced the Spirit's power. They received and gave prophetic words. They saw spiritual gifts used well. They got to "be in the room" when people were healed of pains and delivered from tormenting spirits. They experienced the physical touch of the Spirit's "filling" much like what we read in our Testaments. They got both great information and they got stories to tell. The combination of truth and power has given all four of our kids a vigorous faith that has persevered and matured through the shaking of university, singleness, marriage and parenting. As we look back, we are so glad for what a Word-Spirit life of truth and experience has done for our children.

If you are exploring a more supernatural life with Jesus, my earnest encouragement to you is simple: Just go by the Book! Add nothing. Take nothing away.

Roc Bottomly

July 2019

INTRODUCTION

For many of us who know a lot – or even a little – about God, there is a gnawing, recurring sense that there should be more to our experience with God than what we are seeing.

Our sense is heightened when we read the Bible. On most pages, we read stories about God "breaking in" by speaking, providing, protecting, healing, delivering, and giving supernatural power.

And the results of God's showing up in the stories are wonderful. People rejoice as faith is ignited and they realize – often for the first time – that God is real after all. People devote themselves to Jesus as they realize that His Gospel of forgiveness and eternal life is God's message to us all. People are healed from the pain and disability of agonizing injuries and diseases. People are freed from the overpowering misery of tormenting demons. People are encouraged, amazed and converted through prophetic words that reveal the secrets of their hearts. People find themselves exclaiming in wonder, "God is surely among you!"

When we see these kinds of things happening repeatedly among God's People, we can't help wondering, "Is there more to life with God than what I'm experiencing?"

"Why am I not seeing what I am reading?"

"Where are my miracles? Where is the promised power in my life? Where are the encounters that allow me to testify from firsthand experience that God is undeniably there, His gospel is irrefutably true, and His miraculous power is at work here and now?"

"Can I actually experience what I read in the Book I love?"

The answer, of course, is a resounding "Yes!"

And the way back to the kind of supernatural life and ministry we see in the Bible is to reclaim the full measure of the promised power of the Holy Spirit.

The pages of the Bible clearly promise that when we give ourselves to Jesus Christ we are given wonderful, life-changing power through the Holy Spirit. Through the Holy Spirit, we are promised mental power to understand "the mind of Christ" and the truth God reveals in the Scriptures. We are promised moral power to "put to death the deeds of the flesh" and break patterns and addictions to the evil that disfigures us and damages those we touch. We are promised verbal power to know when to speak and what to say to help others find and follow God. We are promised impact power to bring spiritual awakening and lasting change to the lives of those we try to help. Many of us have experienced these wonderful, life-giving aspects of the Spirit's power.

But there is more.

The Bible also promises that the Holy Spirit gives us miracle power – the power to do supernatural "works" similar to what Jesus did. The power to heal the sick, the authority to free the demonized, the ability to hear God speak to us and through us to others, and the gifts that make God's supernatural presence plain to all... the Scriptures promise all these to all who receive the Holy Spirit by faith in Jesus. And when we live into the promised power of the Spirit, we experience those same wonderful benefits we see in our favorite Bible stories. We see the suffering and tormented set free. We see unbelief become faith. We see lethargy become zeal. We hear visitors in our churches say, "God is surely among you!"

How good is this? It's very good!

But for a variety of reasons (reasons we will explore together), much of our experience with the miracle power of the Holy Spirit has been lost to many today. The good news is that through a variety of influences (influences we will also explore together), God is giving it back!

This book is the story of my journey from knowing God through the truth of the Bible to experiencing Him through the power of the Spirit. My purpose is to encourage those who love the Bible to pursue the full measure of the power of the Holy Spirit promised in the Book they love... and in the process recover the regular experience with God that so invigorates life and ministry.

If you are like most believers raised in the evangelical tradition, your experience of God is rooted in the truth of the Bible. You love the Scriptures. You have studied them diligently, either as a child in Sunday school or just recently in a Bible study. You know the names of all the books in the New Testament and most in the Old. You've memorized treasured verses. You know the stories.

In fact, you have probably been faithfully attending church and studying the Bible for years, doing everything you know to do to bring about a powerful, personal encounter with our heavenly Father.

Yet maybe, just maybe, you sense that *something is missing.* You realize that much of the time you feel discouraged, ineffective, and uncertain. You sense that there's got to be more to life with God than what you've heard proclaimed, seen in the people around you, and personally experienced.

Maybe, if you're honest, you're asking yourself (because you dare not ask anyone else), "Is this all there is?"

In short, the answer is "No!" There is much, much more.

I know how you feel. For years I struggled with the same fears, frustrations, and doubts. I too felt that something was missing yet had no idea what it was.

Eventually, however, God took me on a journey that opened my eyes to pieces of life with Him – promises that were there all along in the pages of the Bible I trusted and loved. I climbed up a high wall, peeked over the top, and saw another part of the Church. From the "Word Church" I peered in to the "Spirit Church" – the part of the Body of Christ that understood, valued, and pursued the promised power of the Holy Spirit. They were doing things that in the past I had intentionally avoided and dismissed as phony or frivolous. Healing sickness. Expelling demons. Hearing God's voice. Exercising spiritual gifts. Worshipping with extravagant affection. To be honest, all these things looked strange and felt uncomfortable…but they matched what I was reading the Book.

I was skeptical, but drawn – drawn by the Scriptures and my desire to experience what I was reading.

Yet despite my skepticism, God patiently showed me that these strange events occurring among believers in the Spirit Church were neither phony nor frivolous. They were important missing pieces in a puzzle I'd been trying to put together all my life.

I had the pieces from my roots in the Word Church that gave me the truth of the Bible, but I was missing many of the pieces that provided the power of the Spirit. When at last I began working with *all* of the pieces, I found myself genuinely experiencing God and His power in a more vivid way. I discovered precious pieces that I needed to more fully know Him, worship Him, and love Him.

Today I have a new awareness of what our awesome God is doing with His church, with His people, and with me. This incredible journey has renewed my enthusiasm for my faith and connected me to a powerful spiritual movement that is spreading to every corner of His Kingdom. In short, it has changed my life in a very happy way.

As we explore it together, I pray it will do the same for you.

CHAPTER 1

A WHOLE NEW FLOOR

I had been a pastor for years, but I'd never seen anything like this.

It was June of 1990, and I was in Kansas City with my wife, Bev, and our two best friends, John and Jan Bingaman. We'd met outside the downtown civic center in the city's famous Plaza district. The spray from rows of sparkling fountains provided welcome relief from the summer heat. When we entered the main hall, we viewed thousands of seats stretching up to the rafters. The place was nearly filled to capacity.

We were there as part of a Passion for Jesus conference. It began with a worship service, and the worship was . . . well, expressive. People raised their hands. At times they clapped and shouted, and some even danced. Others simply stood and wept. A few knelt or lay on the floor, facedown, hands outstretched. They were led by a worship team that at the time looked novel, though today is quite normal: three or four vocalists and a group of musicians playing electric guitars, keyboard, and drums. They pounded out a loud, pulsing rhythm that bounced off the walls around us.

I'd been around a few small worship gatherings that were enthusiastic, but nothing on the scale of five thousand people at once. I was uncomfortable, not only because of the overwhelming size and volume of the whole thing, but also because I was uneasy with intense, open feeling in just about any setting.

I was way out of my comfort zone.

Yet I was also very glad to be among these exuberant worshipers, for this was exactly the reason we'd come — to try to understand what was happening here that was so different from anything we'd known.

So despite our uneasiness, my wife and I decided to give this strange worship style a try. We separated from our friends, the Bingamans, by fabricating some excuse to leave our seats. Neither Bev nor I wanted to be seen raising our hands by anyone we knew. Doing this alone would be awkward enough; allowing our friends to observe us would border on humiliating.

We climbed to the civic center's upper deck and positioned ourselves at the periphery of the crowd where no one would be behind us. After several songs, we finally worked up the courage. Bev went first. I was mildly embarrassed at her public display. Then again, she was a woman — she also giggled, cried, hugged people, and kissed our children. Raising hands wasn't that far out of character and didn't seem quite so excessive for her. It took me a bit longer.

Finally, I did it—only one hand at first, but I got it up. I struggled with the meaning. What is the biblical significance of raising hands? What were the guys in the Bible saying by doing it? I wonder if all these people really know what they're doing. I wonder if they really mean it.

I didn't come up with any clear answers. I felt silly. My mind couldn't justify what my body was doing. I didn't have words to explain it to myself. I imagined trying to defend my behavior to my friends at home. Still, I knew that many others had done this during biblical times. Finally, with my emotions still in turmoil, I raised my other hand so that both were up. Neither reached higher than my ears.

While all this was happening, our friends became concerned. John Bingaman began a search through the building for us. At the precise moment that Bev and I finally got both hands in the air — hers fully extended and mine at ear level — he found us.

"What are you guys sitting up here for?" he yelled above the music. "We saved you great seats at floor level!"

Bev and I were mortified. We'd been caught raising hands in worship! Feeling sheepish, we followed John back down to our "choice" seats. We finished the worship set. I alternated between folded arms and hands in my pockets.

And my unusual day was just beginning.

We returned to the auditorium that evening to hear Mahesh Chavda, a speaker from India. After his message on the compassion and power of God, he invited anyone who wanted healing prayer to come forward. Many came forward, forming a long row in front of the platform. One by one, Mahesh stopped in front of each and prayed quietly. With some he spent considerable time, with others just seconds. Some he touched, laying his hand on the sick places of their bodies. Others he didn't.

As I watched, I noticed a variety of responses. Nothing seemed to happen with some. With others, there was indication of some, but not total, relief. But with many — more than I'd imagined — there was stunning impact. Some fell, lying unconscious — "overcome in the Spirit" — for thirty minutes to an hour. Others later testified of being completely healed of long-standing eye, ear, neck, and back ailments.

I had heard my share of horror stories about false promises of healing and their faith-shattering impact on naïve believers. I had heard of the greedy quacks who had exploited so many in past decades and of the sincere but "uneducated" pastors and lay people who believed that some were still gifted to heal. I'd even seen a few examples of people who professed to be healed after someone had laid hands on them, but I remained skeptical. Yet here I was, seeing firsthand the Spirit "come with power" and people being healed in answer to prayer — or so they said.

Still, I wondered. Does God really do this? Does the Spirit really touch people in a tangible way? Do people really get healed — even sometimes — in answer to prayer?

A month later I got my answer.

"I Think I'm Healed"

In July, the Bingamans were on their way to visit Bev and me in Colorado. Along the way, they returned to Kansas City for a Sunday morning worship service at what was then Kansas City Fellowship. Again, Mahesh Chavda was speaking and praying for the sick. This time, the Bingamans' teenage son, Brock, took his younger brother Joshua by the hand and worked his way through the crowd to the line of people receiving prayer. Ten-year-old Joshua had long suffered from asthma and required strong doses of inhalants daily. When he missed his treatments, his attacks were frequent and severe. Joshua had no idea what to expect. He had never been prayed for in this way. He just stood there with Brock. Eventually, Mahesh approached the pair. Without even touching Joshua, Mahesh prayed a few words quietly and asked him to cross his arms across his chest, breathe in deeply, and then exhale. Suddenly, Joshua fell like a tree. He lay on the floor and appeared to be unconscious.

When John and Jan saw what happened, they rushed to the front and knelt alongside their son. They waited and prayed that God would do whatever He wanted to do with Josh.

Finally, nearly thirty minutes later, Joshua stirred, rubbed his eyes, and asked, "What happened?" He remembered nothing after Mahesh's prayer except feeling "strangely peaceful."

Joshua got up and said simply, "I think I'm healed."

When the Bingamans arrived at our home in Colorado, Joshua told us what had happened in his simple ten-year-old way. I had my doubts, but I was struck by the fact that Joshua was so small, so young, so unexpectant, so unpreconditioned. This was not an adult who had seen others swoon and had thus developed a hope in healing. This was a little kid as new to "things of the Spirit" as I was!

In the days that followed, the Bingamans kept Bev and me up to date on Joshua's status. They decided to try a day without inhalants.

Then a second day.

Then a third. Then a week.

As the days went by and Joshua played happily without medicine and without wheezing, we all felt the same sentiment that follows so many healings in the Gospels: "Everyone was amazed and gave praise to God" (Luke 5:26).

Joshua never took inhalants again. And he never had another asthma attack.

I, on the other hand, did feel under attack — or at least I had the sense that my spiritual past was being challenged.

More than ever, this was a time to think and pray.

Up the Stairs

My experience in Kansas City and my observation of Joshua Bingaman's healing led me to a crossroad. What did it all mean? What was God trying to tell me?

Being compulsively cautious, I wasn't ready to say. It was all too new, too fast, too much, too different from what I'd been saying and doing for so long. I had grown up spiritually in an evangelical environment — that is, I was (and still am) among those who believe in the five fundamentals of biblical Christianity:

1. The authority of the Bible

2. The deity of Christ

3. The rebirth through and empowering by the Holy Spirit

4. The need for conversion by personal faith in Christ

5. The priority of evangelism

You could say that I was a Word person. My faith was rooted primarily in truth, reason, and intellect rather than in power or emotion. Now, however, I'd been exposed to another way of experiencing God. You've probably heard the term many use for this approach: *charismatic.*

I'd heard whispers and been warned about these charismatics before, of course. But now I was in their midst, observing and even participating in their worship, prayer, and healing.

It was exciting, confusing, and a little frightening, all at the same time. The feeling reminded me of the day I discovered my grandmother's attic when I was six years old. While exploring in her home, I came across a door I'd never opened before. I expected another closet. When I turned the latch and pulled, however, I was confronted with a steep, narrow staircase. The air was musty and pungent with the scent of mothballs. The faint diffusions from one small attic window far overhead shed a dim light on the steps.

Curious and frightened, I crept up the creaky stairs, pausing to peer and listen at each step. After what seemed an interminable climb, I walked into a new world of wonderful mysteries beyond my imagination. Surrounding me were old sea chests filled with my grandfather's army uniforms and boxes of military insignia and ribbons; several pairs of mildewed brown riding boots, saddles, and bridles from my mother's childhood; cracked mirrors on dressers with half- opened drawers; a fox stole hanging from a rusty clothes rack, the fox's beady eyes staring at me; my uncle's West Point uniform and his M1 rifle hanging from a nail in one of the wall studs.

Most fabulous of all was a small metal chest filled to the brim with brass soldiers made in China. There were dozens of them posed in a variety of positions — some marching, others shooting.

I'd discovered a whole new floor of the house, a place full of fascinating mysteries. As strange and spooky as they were, there was also something wonderful about those things. From that day on, whenever we prepared for a visit to Nana and Deedee's house, what I looked forward to most was visiting the attic and the forgotten treasures stashed there.

"These things must be worth millions," I'd whisper to myself. "I wonder if there's any way I can get them to give this stuff to me."

That's the way I felt about my new experiences in Kansas City and elsewhere. They were fascinating. Frightening. Invigorating. And somehow, I sensed, worth millions.

Again I wondered, *Is there any way I can get them to give this stuff to me?*

In reality, I had more questions than answers. But one thing was obvious. In the house we call the church, I'd discovered a whole new floor that I'd heard only vague rumors about. And it seemed to offer something I desperately needed.

I had to know more.

Starting the Journey

Have you too — out of curiosity, frustration, desperation, or the urgings of the Spirit — been exploring what it means to know and experience God? Have you even opened that mysterious door, crept gingerly up the stairs, and stared with a combination of fear and fascination at things such as supernatural healings, long- lost spiritual gifts, and extravagant worship? Despite what you may have heard or been taught about these things in the past, have you felt a strange pull to learn more about what God has to say regarding these unusual yet undeniably biblical realities?

You may be ready to embrace this new approach to God with open arms. But if you're at all like me, it's taken a long time for you to decide to even *look* for that mysterious door, let alone start up the stairs.

My own spiritual journey began in a place that was nothing like that freely expressive conference in Kansas City. In fact, it started in a buttoned-down government institution in Colorado, otherwise known as the U.S. Air Force Academy.

Let me tell you about it.

CHAPTER TWO

FILLING THE VOID

As a young boy, I often watched my fighter-pilot father take off in his fully loaded jet and head for the bombing range. His four-ship formation would taxi out to the runway. After a quick check of the gauges, the leader would nod his head, all four pilots would shove their throttles forward, and their afterburners would explode with a deafening roar. I'd keep my eyes on them until the four trails of smoke disappeared into the distant sky.

With these vivid memories, it's not surprising that from my early years I wanted to follow in Dad's footsteps and be a fighter pilot. When I was a high school senior, I got the letter about my potential appointment to the Air Force Academy and immediately ripped it open. I was in!

From the beginning, I loved the Academy. I loved the camaraderie of being with 3,300 other men, living and marching and training together. I loved the structure — every day from reveille to taps packed with a nonstop mix of classes, military training, study, and athletics. And I loved The Code: "We shall not lie, steal, or cheat — nor tolerate among us those who do."

My plan was simple: major in engineering, go to pilot school, build up jet flying hours as quickly as possible, go to test pilot school, and apply for the astronaut program. It was an energizing dream fueled by news of Alan Shepard's first space flight, President Kennedy's commitment to be the first to the moon, academy- inspired ambitions, and my dad's enthusiastic, "Go for it!"

I could not imagine a more invigorating future. But completely unknown to me, something even more exhilarating was waiting for me.

In the second semester of my first year at the Academy, I found myself thrown together with a roommate named Ed Powell. Ed was a cheerful, gregarious companion who helped lift the heaviness of our first-year pressures. What I didn't know was that soon after he came to the Academy, the Navigators found Ed and began to give him some spiritual help.

If you know anything about the Navigators, you know there is no better place to begin your spiritual journey. Throughout their seventy-year history, the Navigators have reached thousands of servicemen, business people, and students in just about every nation of the world. Truly, they have been the pediatricians of the body of Christ. When Billy Graham needed someone to help new converts at his crusades, he called the Navigators. No one takes better care of new believers.

The Navigators believe that we are born to reproduce. Their commitment is to make disciples throughout the world, beginning with the people around them. Well, I was right where Ed was, so he began to pray for an opportunity to talk with me about the things he was learning.

About two months later, he got his chance.

Good News

It was Friday night, and we were getting ready for Saturday morning's "white glove" inspection. We had put Johnson's paste wax on our linoleum floor and were waiting for the buffer to work its way down the hall to our room. As we sat there on a table, Ed asked me straight out, "Have you ever thought much about God and stuff like that?"

"Well, yes, as a matter of fact, I have," I replied. I went on to explain that I believed in God from my years of sporadic church attendance but had concluded that no one could know for sure who He was or what He was like.

"We'll probably all get to see God when we die," I said. "But until then we're all just guessing."

"I've got good news for you," Ed responded. "You don't have to die to know God. He's come to us to show us exactly what He's like. That's what the life of Jesus is all about."

And with that, Ed went on to explain the gospel — the message of forgiveness and eternal life offered in the New Testament to all who turn from wrong and put their faith in Jesus as Savior and Lord.

At the end of our talk, Ed asked me if I was ready to begin that night.

I said, "No. I'm not ready yet." I knew this decision would change the course of the rest of my life, and I wanted to think about it.

About two weeks later, Ed invited me to an Andrew Dinner. Andrew was the disciple who invited his brother Peter to meet Jesus, and this was a dinner set up by the Navigators as an opportunity for Christian cadets to invite their pagan friends to hear about Christ. I was one of the pagan friends and a guest of honor that night.

We met in the upstairs of an old pizza house in Colorado Springs. It was great fun to kick back and eat pizza after the many high-pressured meals in the Academy dining hall. After dinner, one of the instructors in the astronautical engineering department at the Academy, a young captain named Jerry White (later the international president of the Navigators), shared the same message of forgiveness and eternal life I had heard from Ed in our dorm room. The local Dodge-Chrysler dealer then told the story of how trusting Christ had connected him with God and changed his life.

That night it clicked. I vividly remember realizing that Jesus was God in a body, that He died in my place because He loved me, and that He offers me eternal life. After the meeting broke up, I went to a quiet corner of the restaurant and told God I was grateful for how much He loved me and for allowing His Son to die for me. I told Him I wanted to learn more about Him. And I asked Him to help me follow through on my commitment to follow Him all the rest of my life.

That was it. That was how life with God began for me.

It was an amazing night. In some strange way, deep inside I knew I had discovered the God I thought I'd never find, at least not until I died. And I realized at some very deep level, *I'm forgiven. I'm never going to die!* Even at age eighteen, that was an irrepressibly happy thought.

My Spiritual Family

In the Navigator community, following Jesus starts with the Bible. Their philosophy is "You only know God as well as you know His Word."

When Ed found out later that night that I had received Christ, he was delighted — and he insisted that I memorize my first verses. My "spiritual birth certificate" was 1 John 5:11-12: "And this is the testimony: God has given us eternal life, and this life is in his Son. He who has the Son has life; he who does not have the Son of God does not have life." I quickly learned to say it word perfect with the reference before and after.

Within the next week, Ed had me up and reading the gospel of John before reveille. It wasn't long before I found myself in a weekly Bible study looking up verses and filling in the blanks of discipleship booklets. Saturday nights I attended a rally in the local Nav rep's basement and heard him teach the call to live by the Bible. And every weekend I was off to Sunday school and worship at a local Bible-teaching church.

For the next ten years, the Navigators were my spiritual family. They gave me the Bible. They taught me to hear it, read it, study it, memorize it, and meditate on it — to love it and live by it.

Personal time with God and study of the Word were vital, but our spiritual lives were by no means individual. "Man-to-man" was our way of life — an older guy to help each of us younger guys along. This close companionship provided tailored training, encouragement, and accountability. Our study groups of six to eight offered the ideal place to discover and learn together. And our come- one-come-all rallies added rousing music, inspiring preaching, and a sense of movement.

We were a genuine family, a determined band of spiritual soldiers, and a training center of zealots all wrapped into one.

Making Disciples

The wonder of the Navigator ministry is that it seldom turns inward. Our focus was outreach. Woven through all we did privately and corporately was the message that we were following Jesus and that Jesus' last command was, "Therefore go and make disciples of all nations" (Matthew 28:19).

We constantly reminded each other of our mission. Witnessing to our roommates, classmates, teammates — whomever God placed near us — was the privileged work of every disciple. It was what we were left on earth to do.

"Whom," we'd ask each other, "are you leading toward Jesus? Of the new believers, whom are you helping to grow? Whom are you training to 'teach others also'?"

This is my spiritual heritage, and I am deeply grateful for it. From the Air Force Academy, through graduate school at Purdue University, and through my military years at various bases, the Navigators were my spiritual family. They gave me the best spiritual care and training I could have hoped for. They loved me and provided a matchless foundation for a lifetime of personal growth and fruitful ministry. If I could do it all over again, I would still be "born and raised" in the Navigators.

Can you imagine the impact on our culture — on any culture — if all professing followers of Jesus lived out the basics of spiritual growth: the Bible, prayer, fellowship, and witnessing, all combined with hearts determined to keep Christ at the center and wrapped in a culture of love, joy, and grace?

The Great Commission would be fulfilled. The willing would be saved. The church would be victorious. Life with God would be all it could be.

Or would it?

Something is Missing

Though I had an amazing spiritual foundation forged in an atmosphere of love and grace, after ten years with the Navigators I sensed that something wasn't right. Everything I had was good, yet something was missing.

I remember explaining the gospel to one of my instructors in flight school. Colin was a handsome, mustached fellow from the deep South. He was confident and outspoken and a bit intimidating. We sat at a briefing table waiting for the fog to lift so that we could fly. Minutes turned into hours. During that long, agonizing delay, we often found ourselves so desperate for conversation that we were willing to talk about almost anything. In one of those desperate-for-something-to-talk-about pauses, I told him about my involvement with the Navigators.

"Have you ever thought much about God?" I asked.

"Yeah, I have," he said. "I've thought a lot about God. And I've heard a lot about God. But I've never *seen* Him do anything. I just want to see Him *do* something. I hear people talk about God all the time, but I've never seen anything *happen*."

I didn't know what to say. I thought he ought to know better than to expect to *see* God. I thought everyone understood that we can't see God, at least not now. I thought everyone realized that He's no longer doing the kinds of things He used to do.

Finally I responded with, "I'm not sure I can help with that." Then I invited Colin to my Bible study.

I could tell by the way he hesitated that he felt awkward. He didn't want to hurt my feelings, but he also didn't want to go further with our conversation. He took a deep breath.

"Here's the deal," he said. "I have a barn behind my house. If you ask God to strike it with lightning right now and I go home and find it burned down, then I'll come to your Bible study. Short of that, I'm not interested."

We both knew that Colin's barn wasn't going to burn except by a freak act of nature. I certainly wasn't going to ask God for it because at some visceral level I knew He doesn't play that sort of game.

At the same time, I remember thinking, *Man, I wish God did that kind of thing today! It would be so helpful. It would show Colin that God is real and that His message is true. It would be just like what used to happen regularly in the Bible.*

At a deep level, I was frustrated and confused. I felt strangely handicapped. Words alone were not getting the job done. There ought to be *some* place, if not his barn, I could take Colin to show him that God is real and working in the present. Where, after all, was God's promised power?

Something seemed to be missing — something that was present throughout the Book but absent from me and the good people of God that I knew.

This missing link was vital to effective evangelism as well as to relieving the fear and inadequacy that often plagued me.

I had no idea what "it" was. I had only the vague sense that it wasn't a part of my life and that I had to do something to find it.

My solution for filling this void was to do more of what I was already doing — more prayer, more fellowship, more witnessing, and especially more study of the Word. The Bible, after all, was my foundation. That's why in 1976, after a decade with the Navigators, I "left home" spiritually and headed off to Dallas Theological Seminary.

CHAPTER 3

BIG QUESTIONS

If someone was a passionate follower of Jesus in the late 1970s, Dallas Seminary was the place to be. Many of the teachers who epitomize "Dallas" were there and at the height of their ministries: Drs. John Walvoord, Charles Ryrie, Dwight Pentecost, S. Lewis Johnson, and Howard Hendricks. They all were teaching the Bible and personifying the seminary's motto to "Preach the Word."

At Dallas, I was taught to love the Bible as the precious Word of God. I learned to study it with the precision and respect its inspired, inerrant content deserved. I went through three years of Greek and two years of Hebrew and carefully applied the lexical-grammatical-historical approach to each of the Bible's sixty-six books.

Though I loved everything I was learning, I struggled with several unfamiliar subjects. I wasn't nearly as comfortable with the words and ideas of graduate theology as I'd been with the numbers and problem sets of my undergrad math and science back at the Academy. Before seminary, I'd actually spent most of my academic career trying to avoid reading, writing, and speaking. Now, suddenly, I was facing a life of all three!

Languages particularly befuddled me. I still remember laboring over second-year Hebrew. My only consolation was that I wasn't alone. I found two fellow strugglers, one an ex–Dallas Cowboy's football player and the other a fun-loving wrestler from Campus Crusade's Athletes in Action ministry. Together we strained, groaned, and laughed our way through translations of the Psalms that fortunately never circulated beyond the puzzled review of our instructor. I'm still grateful that Professor Don Glenn was more concerned with grace than truth that summer.

These struggles were the exception, however. My overall academic experience was wonderful. The professors were the best credentialed, most thoroughly prepared, and most engaging I'd ever had. The classes were the finest I'd seen anywhere. I'd often sit down at lunch with other students to talk about our professors and the fascinating ideas they offered. "How did they get all that out of that passage?" we'd ask. "Where did they find the rich meaning of that word?"

In so many ways, my Dallas years were amazing and enriching. I benefited from the life-giving discipline of Bible study under the direction of some of the world's preeminent teachers and from an invigorating atmosphere of love, joy, and grace.

And yet, despite the strong, clear flow of biblical truth, I experienced periodic bouts of uncertainty about my faith and the path I'd chosen. About halfway through my first year at seminary, I wondered if I'd made a terrible mistake in leaving the Air Force. I had left the advantages of my Academy background, the momentum of a strong start in a career of tremendous opportunity, my dream of getting into space, the security of a steady income, and significant benefits such as flight pay and the military's medical and retirement programs. Was this really the path God wanted me to take? Had I really heard God's direction? Was God really *there* for me to hear — or to hear me?

I also found myself questioning some of what I was learning from my seminary instructors.

Dallas theology taught cessationism — the theory that much of the miraculous work of the Spirit ceased with the end of the apostles' ministry and the completion of the New Testament. The seminary's doctrinal statement reads, "We believe that some gifts of the Holy Spirit such as speaking in tongues and miraculous healings were temporary."[1]

Dr. Charles Ryrie, commenting on the gift of prophecy, wrote, "This too (along with the gifts of apostleship, healing, miracles, tongues, interpretation of tongues, and discerning of spirits) was a gift for the founding of the church, unnecessary after that period and after Revelation was written in the New Testament."[2]

Although it was not a prominent part of our classroom instruction, there was a prevailing assumption among faculty and students that these strikingly supernatural gifts of the Spirit and the miraculous signs and wonders so prominent in the New Testament (healing, deliverance from evil spirits, direct messages from God, dramatic judgment on sin) had ceased. They simply weren't available to us today.

The careful method of reading and interpreting the Bible that I learned from Dallas professors, however, revealed a very different picture. Countless biblical promises, commands, instructions, and stories clearly anticipate a powerfully present and active ministry of the Spirit that would cause even visiting unbelievers to "fall down and worship God, exclaiming, 'God is really among you!'" (1 Corinthians 14:25).

Take for instance the following examples:

- Jesus promising dramatic, supernatural power to future believers.

- *"I tell you the truth, anyone who has faith in me will do what I have been doing. He will do even greater things than these, because I am going to the Father." (John 14:12)*

- *"But you will receive power when the Holy Spirit comes on you." (Acts 1:8)*

- Paul extending a clear call to all believers to recognize, understand, pursue, value, and exercise supernatural spiritual gifts — without any sense of anticipation that they were about to cease.

- *Now to each one the manifestation of the Spirit is given for the common good. To one there is given through the Spirit the mes-*

sage of wisdom, to another the message of knowledge by means of the same Spirit, to another faith by the same Spirit, to another gifts of healing by that one Spirit, to another miraculous powers, to another prophecy, to another distinguishing between spirits, to another speaking in different kinds of tongues, and to still another the interpretation of tongues. (1 Corinthians 12:7-10)

- *Eagerly desire spiritual gifts, especially the gift of prophecy. (1 Corinthians 14:1)*

- *Therefore, my brothers, be eager to prophesy, and do not forbid speaking in tongues. (1 Corinthians 14:39)*

- *Do not put out the Spirit's fire; do not treat prophesies with contempt. (1 Thessalonians 5:19-20)*

- James affirming the power of healing prayer.

- *Is any one of you sick? He should call the elders of the church to pray over him and anoint him with oil in the name of the Lord. And the prayer offered in faith will make the sick person well; the Lord will raise him up. (James 5:14-15)*

- Philip, an ordinary believer, driving out evil spirits and healing cripples.

- *Philip went down to a city in Samaria and proclaimed the Christ there. When the crowds heard Philip and saw the miraculous signs he did, they all paid close attention to what he said. With shrieks, evil spirits came out of many, and many paralytics and cripples were healed. So there was great joy in that city. (Acts 8:5-8)*

I discovered many more examples in Scripture. And after seeing all of this in the Bible — the Book I was being taught to study, teach, and believe — I couldn't help asking myself,

"Has the power of the Spirit really diminished?"

"Have some gifts of the Spirit really become obsolete? "

"Have the miracles of the New Testament really ceased?"

"Is the 'power of the Spirit' that is so plainly present in the New Testament church really no longer needed today for evangelism and ministry to the church body?"

Although I understood that both Jesus and His Apostles carried a unique power and authority, I was still puzzled by the questions,

"Why would there be a difference between the ordinary people in the early church and ordinary people (like us) in the church today?"

"Where in the Bible are we taught to expect things to change?"

The Elephant in the Room

One moment from seminary stands out in my memory. Twelve of us — our professor, ten other students, and me — were seated around a long table in a conference room where I was leading a discussion on Luke 5:1-11. You probably remember the story: Jesus' disciples-to-be have fished all night and been skunked. They are exhausted, discouraged, and in a decidedly unreligious mood. To their chagrin, Jesus first uses one of their boats as a preaching platform and then directs Peter and crew to launch a boat, let down their nets, and try again. The result is a miraculous catch, so successful that it nearly sinks two boats. Peter, James, and John were so moved that they "left everything and followed him" (verse 11).

As we talked, it struck me that the point of the story is that Jesus performed a miracle so the disciples would move to a deeper level of faith. The miracle-faith connection seemed obvious, yet no one at our table even suggested a link between seeing God work and deeper faith.

The minutes ticked by, and I became increasingly restless. We talked about how the people crowded around Jesus and His amazing ability to connect with common men and women. We observed that His speaking from the boat revealed His determination to allow all to hear His priceless message. We discussed the futility of the disciples' self-effort in their all-night fishing venture. We affirmed the value of trusting God enough to obey when we sense Him telling us to "let down our nets," even in unlikely places. We recognized God's call for us to move beyond lukewarm religion to unconditional commitment.

But we never mentioned the connection between the disciples' supernatural experience and their leap to total devotion. It was like the elephant in the room that everyone pretends not to notice.

Finally I spoke up. "Do any of you see the real point here? Jesus created this supernatural incident so the disciples would *believe more deeply*." My voice rose with excitement. "We've got to help people experience God! We, they, all of us need to *see* Him working to be certain — certain enough to give ourselves as completely as He demands."

I sat back, anticipating a lively discussion on how we might see God and help others do the same.

Silence.

At last, our professor, sitting next to me, mercifully intervened to end the awkward pause. "Well," he gently injected, "expecting experience with God can easily lead to disappointment, disillusionment, and people losing their faith."

What he didn't say, but certainly implied, was that the kinds of things we read about in the New Testament just don't happen today.

I was stunned. I had a great deal of respect for my professor, but what he said did not make sense to me at all. It seemed to me that encouraging people to expect an experience with God was *exactly* what this passage was all about. But because of my inexperience, I kept quiet. We moved to a different subject.

Later, however, I began to wonder, *Is this what's missing? Is it that I no longer expect to see today what is in His Book? Does it have to do with the ministry of the Spirit? Is it firsthand experience with God Himself?*

As I continued to study the Bible, these thoughts circled in my mind like eagles over a salmon run. But I tried to ignore them. The challenge of a new church was beckoning.

My First Church

After four years in Dallas, I graduated with a master of theology degree and moved to Oklahoma City where I helped start a church that attracted a fascinating mix of young and old. Imagine an elderly group of staunch Presbyterians salted with a few nontraditionals in their twenties, all meeting in a dilapidated Czech polka hall. That was Covenant Community Church in its infancy.

Covenant was a strong Bible-teaching congregation with a warm heart and a "come one, come all" spirit. They were master gatherers and winsome people lovers. The church grew quickly. They invited outsiders, followed up new believers, and mobilized laymen into ministry as well and as warmly as I had ever seen it done. I got my first look inside a local congregation with ministries to all ages, compassionate care, and lifelong relationships. This happy spiritual gathering became my family, calling, and profession for the next ten years.

Yet as happy as I was with the way things were moving, I again found myself with a growing sense that something was missing in my relationship with God. I felt there had to be something more. I was stuck.

I loved my work as an expository preacher. But periodically that something-is-missing feeling would surface. Most of my sermon series were book studies: I'd preach through Genesis or the letters of Paul or one of the Gospels.

As I taught from the Gospels, I ran across accounts of Jesus healing the sick, raising the dead, expelling demons, and prophesying comfort and warning. I asked myself, *What should I say about this to my people? Is all of this simply historical information with symbolic implications? Or is any of this a practical example for direct application among us today?*

I taught the story of Jesus healing blind Bartimaeus and thought, *Of course the point here is that Jesus brings the light of truth to a dark and blind world. But is there any suggestion that He heals blind people now? Is there any suggestion here that as His followers today, we should pray for the sick in His name and expect healing? Should I even mention the possibility that we try?*

From the book of Acts, I taught the stories about the early believers healing the sick, raising the dead, expelling demons, and prophesying personal messages from God to those around them — often with the result of bringing enormous relief to those in pain and changing the minds of unbelievers from skepticism to faith. Again I wondered, *Should I say more about these things? Are any of these stories designed to show us how to respond to the pain in our congregations and communicate the reality of God and His love to the unbelievers in our communities? Or is it all just history about what God used to do and foreshadowing of what He will do at the end of the age?*

In my preaching and teaching, I often noticed an uncomfortable difference between them back then and us today. I usually avoided any suggestion of direct application and explained the "deeper meaning" because that's what I'd been taught to do and that's what was expected. But my internal questions continued: *Are we missing something . . . something really important . . . something that would release among us who profess faith the same level of confidence, connection, and courage we see among the people in the Book? What if God is still doing this stuff — even some of it? What would happen if we tried some of these things right here?*

You get the picture. I wrestled and wondered on a regular basis.

My solution was simply to try to live without it — whatever "it" was. Though life with God often seemed distant and incomplete, I concluded that my chronic spiritual aches and questions were just part of the futility and "groaning" that God intends us all to endure until The Curse is lifted.

And besides, like everyone else in our hurry-up society, I was busy. The daily pressures of pastoring pulled me from Sunday to Sunday, sermon to sermon, elders' meeting to leaders' retreat, and wedding to funeral. When would I have had time to think, to look closely at what was and wasn't happening to me spiritually? Despite myself and my schedule, however, I *did* think about it. And in those rare, reflective moments, I began to notice that the wonderful people around me were facing painful struggles for which our vigorous ministry of teaching the Word was simply not giving much relief.

Partially Assembled

Janet, the wife of one of our ministry leaders, battled a chronic and often-suffocating fear that one of her children would die of some terrible disease. She regularly told herself and others, "I guess I'll just have to live with it because there's nothing that can be done."

Devon, a deeply committed and otherwise mature Christian, lived with an overpowering suspicion that his wife would be unfaithful to him. When he saw her talking to another man, he often assumed it was a romantic conversation. The woman had no such intentions, yet his jealous accusations were relentless.

Larry, a devout regular, suffered from recurring bouts with depression. I suspected it stemmed from chronic job conflicts and career disappointments. Whenever the subject came up, he deflected the conversation to something else by laughing it off and saying, "Well, life is just tough all around."

Others were pinned down by addictions to pornography, alcohol, prescription drugs, eating disorders, and consuming work habits. When I slowed my hectic pace enough to notice, I realized that many in my thoroughly orthodox, deeply devoted congregation were, like me, stuck. Some were in dark pits of emotional and relational breakage. Others had become stranded on plateaus of dryness and disappointment with God. Many of us were struggling — often privately, secretly, heroically — not wanting others to know lest they become discouraged themselves.

Like me, these friends, the members of my flock, seemed to be searching for something they didn't have. They believed, yet there was a void in their spiritual life that they couldn't seem to fill.

It was during this time that, with God's help, a vital truth began to dawn on me. I can best explain it with a story.

Imagine that you're working on a jigsaw puzzle in your dining room. The box shows a beautiful scene of a house in the country. The finished picture will include a white two-story colonial home, a velvet green lawn, a shimmering lake, and a herd of cows grazing contentedly in a distant field. It's a wonderful, peaceful setting, the kind of place where you'd like to spend a week — or maybe a year!

You have one thousand puzzle pieces scattered across your table. The border is finished, as well as the house, but most of the interior still needs to be filled in. Fortunately, you've set aside the rest of your day to work on it. You know that when you're working with a thousand pieces, puzzles take time.

Then — surprise! — your spouse announces that company is coming that evening. You'd forgotten all about it. And you'll be having dinner on the dining room table. Your puzzle, your work-of-art in the making, has to move.

Ever try to transfer a partially assembled puzzle from one location to another? It's harder than it looks! But you've got to try. So you find a flat piece of cardboard, place it next to the table, and oh so carefully slide the finished portion onto the new platform.

In the process, several pieces fall on the floor. But that's okay — you'll pick them up later. On your way to the puzzle's new home, a card table in the bedroom, you bump into a wall. A few more pieces fall off the cardboard and scatter. Oh well, you'll get those later too.

Now it's back to the dining room for the pieces that hadn't been connected yet. Your spouse is already setting the table for dinner, so you've got to hurry. You scoop all the pieces in sight into the box, pick up a few pieces off the floor, and dump them next to the puzzle on the table in the bedroom. Your puzzle looks a little worse for the wear, but at least you're ready to begin working again, and you've still got all the pieces you need to finish the picture.

At least, you think so.

Gaps in the Picture

Here is what jigsaw puzzles have to do with questions about our spiritual life with God. As we live and grow and seek a closer relationship with Him, we are like partially assembled jigsaw puzzles. God has told us the picture is going to be beautiful, and we have at least some idea of what it's going to look like. But the picture isn't complete. We need to keep working at the puzzle, adding pieces that bring clarity and purpose and meaning to the picture as a whole. Every piece brings us nearer to God and closer to His purpose for our lives.

The problem is that in the process of journeying through our life and putting together our puzzle, we often drop or forget or overlook pieces of our lives with God. Our picture begins to fill in, but there are gaps. We realize that something is wrong.

Some of the pieces are missing.

That's what happened to me during my years with the Navigators, at Dallas Seminary, and at Covenant Community Church. I was eager to move forward in my spiritual life and in my relationship with God, but the further I went, the more I began to suspect that I didn't have everything I needed to finish the picture.

How about you? Are you missing pieces for your spiritual life or relationship with God? If so, do you know what they are or where to find them? Do you feel as if these missing pieces are stopping you from becoming the person God intends you to be?

As I pondered this concept of missing pieces, I decided I needed to find out more. I wanted to know if others had experienced gaps in their life with God. I wanted to know if there was a history behind this idea of spiritual missing pieces.

Let me show you what I discovered.

CHAPTER 4

PATTERNS OF MISSING PIECES

Because I was a Word guy, I began my investigation of the history of spiritual missing pieces with the Bible. It wasn't long before I came across the story of Josiah. Maybe you're familiar with it.

Josiah assumed the throne of Israel's southern kingdom, Judah, in 640 BC (see 2 Chronicles 34:1). For nearly three centuries, Judah had endured recurring bouts of spiritual jostling. Up and down, back and forth the nation had banged along. You could say that Judah's puzzle had been moved many times. It was shaken during transfers between good and bad kings, faithfulness and idolatry, revival and apostasy. It was bumped by the thoughts and customs of its idolatrous neighbors. The past sixty years had been particularly jarring under the debauchery of Josiah's father, Amon, and his grandfather Manasseh. Worship of false gods, human sacrifices, sorcery, and divination were common practices.

In the course of all this moving and shaking, Israel lost a piece of their life with God. It was a rather significant piece.

They lost the written Word of God.

No one read the Word anymore. No one missed it. In fact, with the possible exception of a few priests, no one even knew it ever existed! For the people of Israel, a huge chunk of life with God was missing.

Think about it. The "People of the Word" had lost the Word. They had lost God's written record of the Beginning, of His covenant with Abraham and the birth of their nation, of the Exodus and the Law of Moses and the wilderness and the conquest and the Promised Land. They had lost the psalms of David and the proverbs of Solomon and the prophesies of Isaiah. The nation born and constituted under a Book — whose existence depended on its people knowing and obeying that Book — had lost it!

But watch what happened next.

After the death of his father, eight-year-old Josiah became king of Judah. As a teenager, despite his deeply corrupt heritage, he experienced what must have seemed to those around him to be an unexpected and mysterious stirring. Josiah "began to seek the God of his father David" (2 Chronicles 34:3).

At age twenty, Josiah put his growing faith into action. In a radical turn away from the mainstream of his culture, he launched a determined assault against the deeply imbedded idolatry of his day. He smashed idols, tore down pagan altars, and executed the apostate priests.

And still he wasn't finished. Just a few years later, Josiah turned his attention to the temple. It had been desecrated and filled with idols, altars, and sacrifices to Canaanite gods. Plaster was peeling off the walls, cracked stones lined the floors, and cobwebs filled every corner. The people's place of worship looked like a dilapidated warehouse.

Josiah was compelled to "repair the temple of the Lord his God" (2 Chronicles 34:8). He cleaned it out, fixed it up, rededicated it, and restored it as the center of worship God designed it to be.

In the midst of the restoration, probably while rummaging through rubble in a long-neglected back room, Hilkiah the priest stumbled across a dusty copy of a long-lost text. He apparently remembered stories of such a sacred scroll and recognized it for what It was – "the Book of the Law of the LORD that had been given through Moses" (2 Chronicles 34:14).

Hilkiah gave the book to Shaphan the scribe, a leading official in Josiah's court. Shaphan was a learned man, an expert in the religion and politics of his day, yet he had no idea what he was holding. Instead of taking the book directly to Josiah, Shaphan decided he'd better review it first to make sure it was worth passing on. Incredibly, even after reading it, Shaphan didn't understand the book's importance. He mentioned it to Josiah only as an afterthought in a business report. In what must have been the understatement of his age, Shaphan said to Josiah, "Hilkiah the priest has given me a book" (2 Chronicles 34:18).

"A book" – good grief!

Fortunately, Josiah directed Shaphan to read to him from this book. The words were completely new to Josiah. No one had ever told him about this text — not his parents, not his teachers, not the leading officials of his court, not even the religiously expert priests and Levites he had reinstated to lead his vigorous spiritual reforms.

No one in Josiah's sphere had ever mentioned anything about this rather significant missing piece of spiritual life. They didn't know what it was. They didn't know what it provided. They didn't know what to do with it. They didn't comprehend its relevance to their individual and corporate survival.

But the more Shaphan read, the more Josiah understood. He began to see that as a nation, Israel had neglected and discarded a precious part of its heritage and life with God. So Josiah repented of his father's rejection of what God had given them. He tore his robes and inquired about the consequences of his people's neglect. He called his leaders and people together, read to them from the lost book, and urged them to take back this missing piece.

Fortunately, the leaders and people responded. They recognized this discovery for what it was—the Word of God. They followed Josiah in his wholehearted commitment to trust and obey it. They renewed their covenant. They removed the trappings of idolatry that were polluting their land. They further restored the temple. They reinstated the priests and Levites to their proper prominence. They celebrated the Passover with an extravagance unmatched even by David and Solomon.

Once again, the nation of Israel experienced heartfelt worship, a vibrant spiritual life, and genuine fellowship with God. Most important, ""As long as he (Josiah) lived, they did not fail to follow the LORD, the God of their fathers" (2 Chronicles 34:33).

A History of Lost Pieces

This story of Josiah and the transformation of the people of Israel was exciting to me because it seemed to fit my developing theory about spiritual missing pieces. So I decided to dig deeper. I wanted to see if I could find other examples of missing pieces in history.

What I discovered is that pieces of our spiritual jigsaw puzzle have been disappearing since the beginning of time. Throughout history, entire generations have grown completely oblivious to vital pieces of life with God:

- By the time of Noah, mankind had lost all sense of righteousness.

- By the time of Abraham, the whole world had forgotten that we are to worship one God and that marriage is monogamous.

- During the time of the judges, Israel forgot about its assignment to conquer Canaan, its Promised Land.

- By the time of Isaiah, heartfelt religion had disappeared. All that remained was empty ritual, which was considered to be completely sufficient.

- By the time of Christ, the promise of a suffering, serving Messiah had vanished so completely that no one — friend or enemy — was able to seriously entertain the possibility.

- Among the first-century Pharisees (the most biblical and devout people of their day), the priorities of mercy, repentance, and faith had dimmed to a flicker, and the need to be born again had completely vanished.

- Among the early disciples, God's call for Israel to be His light to all nations was completely lost.

- By the time of Martin Luther, the church had forgotten that salvation comes by faith.

- By the time of John Wesley, there was no awareness that God wanted His gospel proclaimed to all — especially to those outside church walls.

- By the time of William Carey and Hudson Taylor, the idea that anyone should leave home and actually go to unbelievers in other nations was thought to be ludicrous.

- Until the twentieth century, the church had overlooked the prominent biblical declaration that all believers are ministers who are called to know the Scriptures, evangelize the lost, and disciple others.

Think of it! At different times in our history, we have seen whole communities — even entire generations — completely forget about right living; the concept of one God; monogamy; the Bible; a sacrificing Savior; mercy, repentance, and saving faith; spiritual rebirth; the call to take the gospel to all nations; and the priesthood of believers.

These are not small pieces. Too often, these significant chunks of life with God have disappeared from our corporate memory for centuries.

When I first came upon this revelation, I was appalled. How could this happen? How do whole chunks of truth and practice vital to life with God simply disappear?

Then I began to look back at my own journey. The harder I looked, the more I started to notice several gaps in the picture of my life. I realized that it's much easier to lose pieces of our spiritual puzzles than I had thought.

I have put together a list of some of the ways these pieces can disappear. I'll bet you can identify with at least some of them.

Culture

Culture is a powerful force, much more able to mold and intimidate us than we like to admit. Significant pieces of spiritual life are often culturally unacceptable. Some of God's clearest directions are so universally ridiculed, mocked, and discredited that many of us find them nearly impossible to take seriously. Reserve a day each week for a Sabbath rest — *Who has time?* Pass up a promotion in order to spend more time with God and family — *But we need the money!* Avoid sexually suggestive or explicit movies and television shows — *But everyone else is watching!* Believe in angelic and evil spirits — *surely we've progressed beyond that!*

Culture distracts us from many important pieces of spiritual life. The more immersed we are in the manner of modern times, the less able we are to clearly see God's picture for our lives.

Unwillingness

Sometimes we miss important spiritual pieces simply because we don't accept what is offered. I remember one case when my spiritual mentors were selling, but I wasn't buying. I was urged to attend a Navigator summer program for college students. The focus would be on devotional life and ministry skills — excellent training for a young man still attending the Air Force Academy. I, however, was more interested in going home to visit a girlfriend, so I turned it down. I wasn't willing to rise above what I wanted and pay the price.

Too often, when good things are made available, we simply say, "No thanks."

Devaluation

We may mistakenly underestimate the importance of a particular dimension of spiritual life. Though a piece of spiritual life may be presented in Scripture, we unwittingly toss it aside. Through neglect, it becomes a dusty jewel.

This happened in one of the churches where I was the pastor. Our doctrinal tradition said that the spiritual gifts related to miracles and revelation had ceased with the ministry of the apostles and the completion of the New Testament. After a year of study, however, the majority of our elders concluded that the Bible does *not* teach the ceasing of gifts. The majority agreed that according to what we see in the Bible, we should expect to see all the New Testament gifts in action today. However, that same majority also concluded that the gifts in question — prophecy, healing, miracles, discerning of spirits, spiritual languages and their interpretations — were not important to either a healthy life or ministry. To avoid possible controversy and division within the congregation, it was decided not to teach or pursue these gifts. They were shelved as "things we don't really need around here."

Obsolescence

Obsolescence is similar to devaluation. We see a piece of spiritual life that God clearly commends in Scripture and that past generations vigorously affirmed, but we notice that no one in our circle seems to take part in it anymore. We conclude, "This must be an old piece. It must be for a past age. We must not need it anymore." The piece is considered irrelevant and laid aside. We say to each other, "Yes, God used to do that, but it's not for us here and now."

Look, for instance, at the practice of combining fasting with prayer. Though Scripture clearly shows the great value both God and His people placed in this demonstration of faith (see Joel 1:14; Matthew 6:16-18; Luke 2:36-37; Acts 14:23), how often do we do it today? Don't we as modern believers usually view fasting in particular as a "dinosaur"?

Overreaction

Overreaction is common, especially among protective spiritual communities. We may pursue some clearly legitimate dimension of life with God, but then someone messes it up. It gets abused, misused, mistaught, or misapplied. To protect others from being misled or bruised, leaders often take this piece, put it in a closet, and lock it away. No one is ever wounded by this practice again, but no one enjoys the life-giving benefits either.

This was the approach to sexuality in my spiritual upbringing. During World War II, the Navigators' ministry to U.S. sailors multiplied rapidly. Some of these new believers repeatedly fell into sexual relationships with women in foreign ports. To protect Christian sailors from immorality, the message soon became, "Focus on Jesus. Stay away from women." By the time I came along twenty years later, we were warned that the greatest enemies of our souls were the three Cs: cars, cash, and cuties. This approach led some ministries to nickname the Navigators the "Neverdaters."

Were we protected from distracting or sinful romances? Absolutely. But in the process, we lost a sizeable piece of growing up, and many of us became so socially crippled that we later limped badly in our marriages.

Oversight

Sometimes the people leading and teaching simply overlook a dimension of life with God. They don't see it, so they don't teach it. One generation fails to pass it on to the next. People stop talking about it and start to forget it. Soon a whole community of people is missing something — a piece that may be essential to a complete spiritual life. For example, churches and other ministries focused on the present may neglect our future hope despite its enormous biblical prominence. In the same way, those absorbed in evangelism may disregard the importance of worship or social justice.

Preoccupation

Every spiritual community begins with a calling — an error to correct, a group to reach, a place to go, a mission to fulfill. Often the focus required to carry out our objective screens out other pieces. In the short run, these pieces seem to interfere with our mission. But in the long run, they are vital to our spiritual health.

This was my experience in one of my early ministries. We were focused on recruiting young people to "make disciples of all nations" (Matthew 28:19). As we pursued our calling to reach young, single students through intense weekday ministry in homes and dormitories, we failed to appreciate the Sunday activities and family emphasis offered at the local church. The passionate pursuit of our God-given assignment blinded us to a large piece of basic biblical living.

Personal Preference

Be honest here – aren't you uncomfortable with at least some of the things God commands? You don't understand them. You don't want to discuss them. And you certainly don't want to do them. When the Bible calls you to shout, lift your hands, clap, and dance in worship; to weep and wail in repentance; and to anoint the sick with oil and ask for healing, don't you sometimes find yourself thinking, *I wish it didn't say that?*

Do you ever find yourself selectively following the teachings that make sense to you?

I know I do.

In my spiritual family, there was a strong preference for sound thinking, predictability, control, and learning. On the other hand, we tended to shy away from emotion, risk, mystery, and intimacy. As I'll soon explain, that led to the loss of some vital pieces.

God's Timing

Sometimes our missing pieces are purely the result of God's timing. God graciously reveals new truths to us throughout the course of our lives, but only as we are ready for them. There is more that He has to teach you — many marvelous things about Himself and how He works. They are missing pieces for now because they are part of His future plan.

Does anything on this list sound familiar to you? I'm sure there are many more ways that we drop parts of God's picture for our lives. In fact, the list is probably endless.

You may find that thought discouraging. If it's so easy to miss God's spiritual blessings, you may wonder, what hope is there for me?

Hope of Renewal

The answer is that there is abundant hope: "May the God of hope fill you with all joy and peace as you trust in him, so that you may overflow with hope by the power of the Holy Spirit" (Romans 15:13). God never turns His back on us. Instead, He is ever faithful, patiently pursuing us and continuously holding out the missing pieces we so carelessly misplace.

Look, for example, at how God responded to Josiah and the people of Judah. When He saw the king's willing and obedient heart, God allowed Hilkiah the priest to discover the Book of the Law. He knew that Josiah, despite the mistakes of his ancestors, was ready to lead his people back to embracing the Word of God. Likewise, when His people substituted ritual for compassion and character, God sent the Old Testament prophets with their message to "stop bringing meaningless offerings! ... Stop doing wrong, learn to do right! Seek justice, encourage the oppressed. Defend the cause of the fatherless, plead the case of the widow" (Isaiah 1:13,16-17).

When everyone, including the most educated, forgot the need for spiritual rebirth, God the Son patiently sat with Nicodemus to explain, "You must be born again" (John 3:7).

When the entire organized church forgot that forgiveness of sins and eternal life are free gifts for those who believe, God returned this lost truth through Martin Luther as he read and taught the book of Galatians to his parishioners and theological students.

More recently, when we forgot that ordinary people can evangelize and disciple — often more effectively than professional clergy — God handed back the lost piece of the priesthood of all believers through men such as Dawson Trotman, Bill Bright, and Billy Graham.

These are the stories of a faithful God who says to us, "Hey, you dropped this! It is something you need. It will help you make sense of what is going on. It will help you experience Me and know that I am near. It will help you restore what is crippled. It will set you free. Here, take it back!"

When we listen to God and take back the pieces He hands to us, the result is *renewal*. When we see something about God we never saw before, when we realize that God is willing to do things we never imagined, when we become aware of an avenue of help we never thought was available, there is fresh zeal. A new hunger for God. A new desire for His Word. A new love for His people. A new joy, boldness, affection, energy. A new life!

This is a pattern that replays itself throughout the history of devout people. We lose pieces of life with God. The Lord gives them back. We respond and experience an invigorating surge of renewal. And when the missing piece is big, the renewal is revolutionary.

It's still happening today. Most of us just don't realize it. We're too preoccupied with the difficulties of getting through each day. It's as if we're sleepwalking through our lives, only vaguely aware that something is missing and lacking the energy or direction to get it back.

You could say that I was sleepwalking for many years. I was wandering about in a trancelike state, seeking answers but unable to find them. Then, at last, something changed, and it transformed everything about my life.

I finally woke up.

CHAPTER 5

AWAKENING

My spiritual awakening started with digging deeper into the Word. I had already noticed an enormous gap between what was happening to the people of the Bible and what was happening around me. I decided it was time for a closer look.

In the Bible, with the exception of a few periods of divine judgment when God seems to abandon them, the people regularly experience God in vivid, tangible ways. They hear Him speak directly — at times audibly and at other times through visions, dreams, inaudible promptings, or prophets. They see Him work regularly — miraculously providing, protecting, healing the sick, delivering the tormented. They feel His powerful touch that shakes their meeting places, disciplines the defiant, reveals His plans, and sends His people into eruptions of praise and prophesy.

Look for yourself.

In the very first chapter of the New Testament, we see the Holy Spirit creating a baby in the womb of a virgin, an angel speaking to a man in a dream, and a prophet delivering a message from God — all of which takes place in just three short paragraphs! In chapter 2 of the book of Matthew, we read about a mysterious star leading pagan astrologers to the house of the Messiah, God speaking in a dream to send these men home, an angel appearing in another dream to send Joseph to Egypt, an angel appearing in a third dream clearing Joseph to return home, and an angel appearing in yet a fourth dream leading Joseph to settle in Nazareth.

In chapter 3, we see God personally revealing the Messiah to John the Baptist, the Holy Spirit descending in a visible form, and the audible voice of God identifying His Son. In chapter 4, we witness the Holy Spirit directing Jesus to the wilderness, angels appearing in the aftermath of satanic temptation, people being healed of "every disease and sickness" (verse 23), and tormented demoniacs being set free.

If this description of life with God were confined to the first few chapters of the New Testament or even to the life of Jesus, then we might reasonably say, "That sort of encounter with God was just for those at the time of Christ."

But it's not.

Regular, vivid encounters with God begin with His conversations with Adam and continue in the lives of the faithful throughout the thousands of years of Old Testament history. And these encounters with God continue after Jesus' life throughout the recorded history of the early church (Acts), the inspired letters to those first churches (the Epistles), and the final Revelation in which we find John "in the Spirit" (1:10; 4:2; 17:3; 21:10) — a state common enough among early believers to be easily understood by John's readers.

In fact, throughout the entire biblical record, God is tangibly present doing things that people can see and hear and feel.

Try this little experiment. Randomly open your Bible to any narrative section and read. What do you see? Now try it again.

Unless your results are unusual, here is what you'll find just about every time you open the Book: God appearing, God speaking, God providing, God striking, God protecting — and people describing what they saw and heard and felt of Him. God is being experienced on almost every page.

Now compare what you read with what you see today. If you are even a casual Bible reader, you can't help but notice the enormous gap between what the people in the Book expected and experienced and what's happening around most of us in the twenty-first century.

Either those things never happened back then or God has radically changed His ways between the times of the Book and the present.

Or something is missing, and it's something that provides us with regular, firsthand, vivid contact with God.

Miracles on the Mission Field

My awakening continued as I read and thought about what is happening overseas today. Have you noticed any difference between the church in the mission field and the church at home? I found myself reading about Islamic holy men coming to Christ through dreams, angels appearing to defend Congolese missionaries from murderous guerillas, Filipino churches starting as a result of blind men seeing, Thai ancestor worshipers converting after being freed from tormenting spirits, Chinese house-church pastors being warned through visions about impending raids by the secret police, and even a Nigerian pastor being raised from the dead three days after he was killed in an auto accident.

These accounts seemed to describe a miraculous, very present, and very active God working among people of simple faith.

Then there were the reports from those showing the *JESUS* evangelistic film overseas.

Report 1: A Captain Changes Course

What God is doing here [Burma] brings chills to my back. Earlier in this century, after 100 years of colonial rule, the Burmese rejected anything Christian, including the witness of "Western" missionaries. . . . Then . . . the arrival of God's miracles, and, the "JESUS film!" One "captain" (regional leader) hindered the work of one of the "JESUS" Film Teams. There was no way he wanted this Western film shown in his area. At the same time, his wife became mysteriously ill. For days, she slipped toward death, and finally lapsed into unconsciousness. While in that state, she had a powerful vision of Jesus (whom she had never seen).

I don't know if the illness was natural or from God. In any case, when she regained consciousness, she told her husband what she had seen and urged him to let the Film Team work. He did, and she was instantly healed. She immediately gave glory to Christ, the "almighty God."

Her husband, the captain, also came to Christ and now provides transportation for that same Film Team through the rugged mountains so the film can be seen in remote villages!

In another place, a rather educated woman, who was deeply skeptical of Christianity, was journeying to a village. She looked up and saw a clear vision of Jesus in the sky. She called out to a fellow teacher who was with her to look up at the sky, and that teacher also saw the image. Before, she would not even allow a pastor to set foot in her house. Now, her whole family believes! . . .

I am convinced that behind all this, in the unseen realms, there is a tremendous battle being waged for the spiritual destinies of 45 million Burmese. That's why our national leadership earnestly wants to greatly expand the work, to reach many, many more Buddhists, Hindus, and even Muslims in the area . . . while God is so wondrously at work.[1]

Report 2: Divine Earthquake

In a closed Muslim nation, a Campus Crusade staff couple invited a Muslim husband and wife to their home to watch a video of "Jesus." Even though they were fervently committed to Islam, they agreed. During the film, everything in the room began to shake. Yet, they were so gripped by the video they just kept watching!

Before "JESUS" ended, unknown to the other, each prayed to receive Christ. Fearful of the other's reaction, they returned home, not saying a word about their decisions. The next morning, they couldn't stand it any longer. At great risk, they each told the other what they had done. They wept as they discovered they had both come to Christ.

When they revisited the Campus Crusade couple, they shared how they had both "felt the room shaking with great power." Even though they were the only ones who felt this "divine earthquake," they agreed that at the moment the shaking began, each knew it was a sign from God — His affirming to them of the truth of the film. Today, these once fervent Muslims are helping to translate training materials for Campus Crusade![2]

Report 3: Back from the Dead

The Malto tribe lives in the north of India, in the state of Bihar. The people are resistant, even hostile, to the gospel. It is an area "saturated" with the worship of Satan and hundreds of false gods. The people know their god as Satan, the great evil god, who oppresses them. This is why I believe, *on occasion*, our sovereign Lord uses extraordinary means— miracles — to break down such barriers and validate His truth.

The "JESUS" Film Team approached the Malto tribe. But the resistance was so stiff that they bypassed the area and went on to more receptive villages. A few days later, a sixteen-year- old girl died in one of the Malto villages.

It was evening, the family had finished all the preparations for burial. Many had gathered around to pay their respects and support the family. They were about to bury the body when the girl suddenly, miraculously awoke.

In stunned disbelief the people told her, "Then you are not dead!"

"Yes, I was dead, she told them. " I went to the place of the dead, but God told me I must come back and tell you about the real God, the true God."

Still astonished, the villagers began to ask her, "Then who is the true God?"

She went on to tell them it was the God proclaimed by the Film Team they had turned away.

"God has given me seven days to tell as many people as I can that He is real," the girl said.

The next day, she sought out and found the Film Team in another village. She told them her story and that God had told her she was to go with them. For the next seven days, they showed the film to the now receptive Malto villages. (Needless to say, word had spread everywhere about her return from death!)

Before every crowd she fearlessly proclaimed, "I was dead, but God sent me back to tell you that this film is about the true and living God. He has given me seven days to tell you. You need to believe in Him."

Then, after the seventh day, although physically she appeared fine, she collapsed and died. . . .

The greatest evidence that something wondrous happened is that during those seven days, hundreds of people who were bound by the chains of Satan turned to the living Christ. As a result, six churches were established. Certainly, God was glorified!

As I read these reports, I stopped to consider the implications. Either these miracles weren't really happening over there or God changes the way He relates to people according to geography.

Or there is something missing in our Western, evangelical brand of life with God — something directly related to the presence and power of God.[3]

Spirit People

At this point, God certainly had my attention. But I had another discovery to wake up to — one that was perhaps the most enlightening of all.

It grew out of encounters with Christians who were "not of my kind." These were people from the other side of the ecclesiastical tracks. I knew them as Pentecostals, charismatics, Spirit people.

From the beginning of my Navigator days, I had viewed charismatics as Christians of a completely different kind — almost cultish. Of course, I didn't know many. I had been warned of the dangers of associating with charismatics because of their preoccupation with the Holy Spirit; their misleading ideas and expectations about the power of God; their neglect of the Great Commission and overemphasis on worship; their history of weak character, moral failure, and emotionalism; and their lack of discipline, disregard for education, and devaluing of rigorous Bible study.

Therefore, I usually avoided them as much as possible. I seldom read anything they wrote and never visited the places they gathered.

One Spirit person I didn't avoid, however, was a woman named Betty Owens. When I met her, she was in her mid-fifties and was gray haired, strong, radiant, and a striking combination of Southern warmth and dignity. For the five years I was stationed at a nearby airbase, she and her husband, a physician, hosted gatherings of up to one hundred college students and young military people. Sunday nights at seven was Afterglow; Tuesday mornings at six thirty was Prayer Breakfast, person- ally served by Dr. and Mrs. Owens to all who came.

Mrs. Owens asked several Navigator-trained guys to lead the Afterglow Bible study, which we gladly did (in part, I confess, to experience the rich array of sights and scents provided by the beautiful Georgia girls who regularly attended).

We learned much about the Bible from Mrs. Owens. She knew it inside and out, and she respectfully (but firmly) coached us as we led our studies.

Mrs. Owens also taught us about the Spirit. She had been raised on the mission field in Korea and was keenly attuned to the supernatural world. She understood the power of prayer. When she would not know what to pray, she would pray in languages that no one understood — languages given, she said, by the Holy Spirit. By her account, this kind of praying would often lead to a deep, spirit-to-Spirit connection and to a sense of how God wanted her to pray for the person at hand.

To be honest, I found this whole idea so disturbing that I seldom listened in to find out how it worked. Now I wish I had.

Then there was Dr. Derek Prince, a charismatic New Testament scholar who undid my well-constructed stereotype that "these people are biblically ignorant." His messages on the ministry of the Holy Spirit and spiritual gifts — as well as his teaching on the biblical principles of marriage and child raising — were solidly scriptural and practically illustrated by reliable reports from others who were experiencing what he was teaching. I listened to several of his tape series and thought they seemed reasonable. Yet they were much too different from my familiar ways for me to absorb.

Years later, I periodically came up for air from my frenzied busyness and wondered about my encounters with these Spirit people. Either men and women like Dr. Prince and Mrs. Owens were not really doing what it appeared they were doing, or God visits some people very personally but others not so much.

Or perhaps something *was* missing in my life and the lives of many others, and it was something that regularly brought God near and made Him very real.

Getting Personal

The Bible, the mission field, and these "other kind" of Christians were all saying to me that something was missing. But the closest, most pressing voice of all was my own longing for the personal relationship with God that I had been hearing about and promising to others from the beginning.

Personal relationship. It means Him and me tangibly connected. It means not just imagining but seeing. It means not only talking to but hearing from. It means getting not only the mass mailing of Scripture but also the special deliveries of personal messages. It's the fellowship with God — the *koinonia* — repeatedly promised in the Bible (see 1 Corinthians 1:9; 1 John 1:3).

The only problem I had with personal relationship was that for the most part, I hadn't experienced it.

I had survived largely by imagining it. By remembering what God had done in the past, I imagined my life continuing what He had started.

By anticipating being with Him in the future, I imagined being in His presence. By knowing that He was omnipresent, I imagined Him being with me and watching over me. To be honest, much of my personal relationship was only in my head. The actual experience — His speaking, His touching, His empowering — was greatly lacking. There was certainly some of it but not as much as I wanted.

Whenever I let myself be honest, I realized I was hungry for God — really hungry.

If the Bible was the plumb line of what is true and what we can expect, I *was* missing something. I was missing whatever it is that brings God near — near enough to hear and see and touch, near enough to experience regularly, near enough to share a genuine personal relationship.

I was trying to fill in my spiritual jigsaw puzzle with imaginary pieces.

The Realization

All my questioning, searching, and sleepwalking led me to an astonishing realization: The Spirit who was so active and powerful during biblical times is just as active and powerful today — at least among those who acknowledge His presence and welcome His working.

I already knew from my study of the Bible that the Holy Spirit is not a thing or a force but a *Person* who thinks (see 1 Corinthians 2:10-11) and feels (see Ephesians 4:30) as we do. Yet at the same time, He is fully God — knowing all (see 1 Corinthians 2:10-11), present everywhere (see Psalm 139:7), holy (see Luke 11:13), the Creator of the universe (see Genesis 1:2), and the Giver of life (see Romans 8:2).

I also understood that the Spirit delivers supernatural power, both *psychological* power (for example, to understand God's truth and to feel His comfort, joy, and peace) and *moral* power (to resist wrong and pursue right). Yet somehow, through a combination of cultural influence, religious heritage, and personal blindness, I'd missed something vital — the Spirit's provision of supernatural *working* power.

The Holy Spirit gives us the ability to do the miraculous works that Jesus did, such as healing the sick (see James 5:13-16) and delivering others from tormenting spirits (see Matthew 10:1-8; 28:18-20; Luke 10:1-20; 11:20). He enables us to know things only God knows (see 1 Corinthians 14:24-25), to prophesy (see 1 Corinthians 14:1), to speak with God spirit to Spirit (see Acts 2; 10; 19; 1 Corinthians 14:1-17), and to receive and use miraculous spiritual gifts for the benefit of others (see 1 Corinthians 12:7-11).

It is through the Spirit that we become family with God — as close as Father and son: "Those who are led by the Spirit of God are sons of God. For you did not receive a spirit that makes you a slave again to fear, but you received the Spirit of sonship. And by him we cry, 'Abba, Father'" (Romans 8:14-15).

I was in the family, but I felt like a second cousin. During all of my years as a believer, I had somehow missed something incredibly important — the full measure of the power of the Holy Spirit. God in me. It was only through the power of the Spirit that I would come to experience God to the extent promised in His Book.

This was the missing piece to my puzzle. It was what I'd been searching for. I realized that God had pursued me, just as He had so many of His children throughout history, and was now holding out my missing piece, the working power of the Spirit. All I needed to do was take it.

It was this realization that woke me from my spiritual slumber. I was finally fully alert, open to going wherever God would lead me to gain a deeper understanding of Him and His power and plan for me. I was ready for the next step.

The question is, "*Are you?*"

CHAPTER 6

CHOOSING YOUR WINESKIN

The fact that you picked up this book probably means that something unsettling has already happened to you. Life with God either isn't what it used to be or it is not quite what you expected. I'm guessing that you feel stuck and discouraged and are just not sure what to do.

Here's the good news: You have arrived at the beginning of your awakening. Because you are already aware that something isn't right — that something is missing from your life — you're right where you need to be, ready for God to open your eyes to a missing piece He wants to give back.

If you hadn't already been pondering the ways we relate to God, the previous chapters have probably nudged you into thinking about it. Like me, you may be in the process of discovering that God has provided us with *two* supernatural forces of staggering value: His Word and His Spirit. Of course, you have loved the Bible and the Holy Spirit for as long as you have followed God. I suspect, however, that you are now realizing there may be much more to one of these — either Word or Spirit, depending on your background — than you ever imagined.

You might say that God is ringing your spiritual alarm clock. The temptation will be for you to hit the snooze button, roll over, and go back to sleep. To fully emerge from your spiritual slumber and hear and respond to the message God wants to teach you, you'll want to adopt what I call attitudes for awakening.

Ready for New Wine

The attitudes you'll need are vividly revealed in Jesus' parable of the wineskins.

The topic is receiving "new wine" — new things God is in the process of teaching His people. The parable specifically speaks to those who embrace what God is doing and to those who reject it.

Read this exchange between the Pharisees and Jesus:

> They said to him, "John's disciples often fast and pray, and so do the disciples of the Pharisees, but yours go on eating and drinking."

> Jesus answered, "Can you make the guests of the bride- groom fast while he is with them? But the time will come when the bridegroom will be taken from them; in those days they will fast."

> He told them this parable: "No one tears a patch from a new garment and sews it on an old one. If he does, he will have torn the new garment, and the patch from the new will not match the old. And no one pours new wine into old wineskins. If he does, the new wine will burst the skins, the wine will run out and the wineskins will be ruined. No, new wine must be poured into new wineskins. And no one after drinking old wine wants the new, for he says, "The old is better."" (Luke 5:33-39)

Jesus' response to the Pharisees begins with a question. On the surface, it seems to concern fasting and prayer. But the parable touches on a deeper matter: Why would God work through the disciples, a group of unconventional and uneducated men from outside the system? Why would He use people who are not saying and doing the "accepted" things? Why wouldn't God stick with religious veterans?

Jesus' answer is simple: Religious veterans generally reject new things.

The new thing God was doing at the time of Christ was not new in the sense that it was unbiblical. God's mercy toward sinners and righteousness by faith had been part of His Word from the beginning (see Adam and Eve in Genesis 3, Abraham in Genesis 15, and David in Psalm 32). But these pieces of foundational truth had been lost. They were missing, bumped from the jigsaw puzzle. They'd been forgotten and were no longer a part of the religious culture of the day. They were not commonly understood, taught, or believed.

In fact, the religious veterans were not just oblivious to mercy and faith.

They actively fought against them.

For God to do the new things He was doing through Christ, He had to find people willing and able to receive an old, forgotten set of ideas (for example, that God loves outcasts and invites them back to Him). He needed to find people with minds and hearts willing to learn new things from God — things not found in the tradition of the day, things not taught in the established religious community.

Where would He find such people?

Many vested in the established religion of the day were unable to adapt. They simply would not and could not make the changes. Something deep inside them insisted that "the old is better." After so many years of drinking old wine, they did not want anything new.

Let's be honest — we too have powerful inclinations to resist change, especially spiritual change. We find it hard to learn new things about God even if they come from God Himself through His Word.

Sadly, tradition trumps Scripture most of the time. There is security in what is known. There is loyalty to those who taught us. There is safety in sticking with the tried and true. There is pride that resists the idea that we've missed or dropped something along the way, especially if it's being offered by those who are younger or from a different spiritual stream.

Most of us tend to be old garments and old wineskins. We don't want to flex, stretch, and accommodate new spiritual pieces. Recognizing, receiving, and responding to God's new wine is a problem for most of us. It's a problem we've got to meet head-on if we are to receive the lost or new pieces of spiritual life that God offers.

Essential Attitudes

So what's the solution? Clearly, from Jesus' parable, heart attitudes are crucial. The same mindset that was essential to the disciples for receiving the New Covenant is essential to us for receiving the benefits of any change God may bring.

These are the attitudes that enabled the disciples to receive the new wine Jesus was pouring into them. If you adopt them, you too will be prepared to receive His sweet and holy instruction.

Humility

If we are going to learn new things from God, we must realize we have new things to learn. So often we tend to think, at least subconsciously, *I have all the pieces. In my spiritual family, we know all there is to know. We have all there is to have. We do all there is to do. Anything outside the circle of our doctrine and practice is either wrong or unnecessary. The theology faithfully passed on by those who taught me contains all that's needed for life and ministry.*

Trust in our spiritual parents, allegiance to our denominational roots, confidence in our familiar theologies, memories of our beloved Sunday school teachers, and respect for our Bible study leaders all encourage loyalty to our traditions. Add to these sometimes intense loyalties our concerns over our personal reputations within our spiritual families and the peace of mind that comes from assuring ourselves that we've been doing and teaching the right thing for so long, and we'll find ourselves bound to our traditions by bands of steel.

All these factors tend to block new truths from us. They subtly conspire to make us proudly unreceptive to anything foreign to what we already "know" to be true.

I recall that in my early years with the Navigators, we were deeply committed to helping people do the here-and-now part of life with God, but we seldom talked about the future — prophecy and the end times. In spite of the unmistakable prominence of future hope in the Bible, I gradually began to think that dwelling on the future was a waste of time that distracted from our primary mission of discipling.

Humility, however, demands a mind and heart that are always open to new lessons from God. Humility's lifelong prayer is,

> Show me your ways, O LORD, teach me your paths; guide me in your truth and teach me, for you are God my Savior, and my hope is in you all day long.
>
> (Psalm 25:4-5)

There is no way we can have all the pieces of His nature, His ways, His plans. There are simply too many. His blessings and teachings will always overflow. Embracing the infinite conveyor belt of new things we have yet to learn in our lifelong pursuit of God is the essence of being new wineskins.

Faith

We must trust the mercy and power of God to lead, help, and protect us. Learning new things about any subject brings fear— of the unknown, of mistakes, of embarrassment, of deception, of exploitation, of failure.

For example, we all tend to fear the Devil and his schemes, which is understandable. He is the master Deceiver. But while caution is warranted, frozen intimidation is not.

When I first began to listen for God's voice, I remember freezing in the gale of two fears. The first was the fear of deception — what if the Devil saw me listening for God and broke in with his counterfeit message? The second was the fear of silence — what if God didn't speak? How embarrassing and disillusioning that would be!

Fortunately, someone reminded me that God is big enough to keep Satan from patching in to His communications, and He is much more willing to speak than I am to listen. In my twenty years of listening for His voice, I can't think of a single message from the Devil that came when I asked God to speak. And the few times when nothing came, it really wasn't that embarrassing to say to the person I was praying with, "I'm not hearing anything at the moment. Let's try later."

Old wineskins are driven by fear. New wineskins are full of faith in the protection, power, and mercy of God.

Risk

Progress in any arena is spelled R-I-S-K. Learning anything new involves risk — taking the chance of doing it wrong, looking foolish, being misunderstood, and the most dreadful of all conceivable consequences, *failing*.

In fact, mistakes are part of God's divine process. Whether we are learning to eat, talk, walk, read, hit golf balls, make a dress, pray for the sick, cast out demons, hear God's voice, speak in a spiritual language, or adore God publicly, each involves trial and error. Each involves stumbling and falling. Each involves missteps and, yes, failure. Each requires the willingness to take risks.

During the 1800s, a man suffered business failures, the death of his fiancée, and a mental breakdown. He also fell short in numerous bids for positions that included state legislator, speaker of the state legislature, presidential elector, state land officer, congressional representative, U.S. senator (twice), and U.S. vice president. Yet Abraham Lincoln learned from his previous failures and ran successfully for U.S. president in 1860. The fortitude he gained from his difficult past helped him guide America through one of its most challenging times. Today, many historians regard him as this nation's greatest leader.

It is only by accepting the uncertainty of risk and the humiliation of failure that we will become new wineskins.

Mystery

Jesus said of the Holy Spirit, "The wind blows wherever it pleases. You hear its sound, but you cannot tell where it comes from or where it is going. So it is with everyone born of the Spirit" (John 3:8).

There is an unavoidable, wonderful mystery to God and how He works. When we toss in our own sin and blindness, the severe limits of our minds and experiences, the curse on creation, and the divinely designed futility of the present age, our ability to understand, predict, explain, and control what happens in our lives drops drastically.

The truth about much of what God does today is simply this: Sometimes He does, and sometimes He doesn't. This applies to healing, speaking, imparting gifts, expelling demons, and igniting revivals. As much as we'd like these things to happen on command, we can orchestrate very little of God and His power. He is present. He is active. He is still very much in the miraculous, wonder-working business. But He is also in touch with many things that we don't understand or see.

In the end, we can ask God to work, we can invite people to receive, and we can create opportunities for Him to move, but we can't manipulate Him into anything. We can't say with certainty, "Today God will heal, impart gifts, deliver, pour out His Spirit, or start a revival." Although we know that He does all these things, we simply can't predict, control, understand, or explain when, where, or how God works.

For most of us, this is uncomfortable. For many, it is unacceptable. When God wants to add mystery to our wineskins, many of us resist, stiffen, and eventually rip apart at the seams.

To embrace a new wineskin is to embrace mystery. We must be able to live with the fact that sometimes He does and sometimes He doesn't and persist through the times He doesn't to ask for and anticipate His powerful working at a later time.

Hunger for the Presence of God

Everyone wants the presence of God, right? In theory, yes; in practice, no.

The problem is that there will always be tension between our desire for God's presence and our desire for propriety. When God unleashes His power and manifests His presence, it can be overwhelming. It can bring mental, physical, and emotional overload. The simple truth is that God is an overwhelmingly awesome God. When He reveals Himself, exposes our hearts, touches our bodies, and teaches new things, we are consistently undone. If touching a hot electrical wire jolts our bodies, imagine what it's like to be touched by God!

Think through the biblical accounts of God's visits to people. What hap- pens when they encounter God? Trembling, shaking, collapsing in a heap, falling on knees, crying out in fear, wailing in repentance, writhing in deliverance, weeping for joy, erupting in praise, proph- esying ecstatically, and seeing celestial visions. When Jesus healed a man possessed by evil spirits, demons spoke and two thousand pigs drowned. The shocked and frightened people pleaded with Jesus to "leave their region" (Mark 5:11-17). When the Spirit came upon the early disciples at Pentecost, there was the sound of violent wind, vi- sions of fire, and the eruption of strange languages. Those at hand were "amazed and perplexed" (Acts 2:1-13). Those touched were accused of being drunk (see Acts 2:13).

God's works can be intense, mystifying, disorderly, and unexplainable.

If we like things quiet, predictable, controlled, and mildly pleasant — and most of us do — we've got to learn to love the presence of God more than neatness and propriety. New wineskins recognize the life-changing, life-giving impact of God's presence, and they are more than willing to live with the life- giving upheaval.

Devotion to the Word

If we are going to stay supple and teachable by God, we must love the Word of God more than our theologies and traditions. Our motto must always be "Just go by the book."

We've got to stay committed to following the example and instruction of the Scriptures. We can't filter out what's unfamiliar or uncomfort- able. We can't change the meaning of passages to fit personal pref- erence or accepted practice. We can't drop things out. We can't add things in.

Just go by the book.

It sounds easy enough. But again, for most of us, it is difficult and rare. Our religious traditions— Baptist, Presbyterian, Lutheran, Nazarene, Evangelical Free, Methodist, Church of Christ, Episcopalian, Catholic, Campus Crusade, Navigators, Young Life, or whatever else it might be— exert a powerfully conforming force.

In most cases, our traditions have provided tremendous good. They have steered us to where we are today. They come from the people who gave us spiritual birth, who taught us all we know, who loved us through the awkwardness of our first spiritual steps. To depart from our traditions is, in a very real way, to disregard those we love. It is to risk losing our place at the table and our relationships with those who are most important to us. The mental, emotional, and relational bonds of tradition are compelling. Often, they are unbreakable.

The result is lots of old wineskins.

To grow beyond the limits of our traditions, to be patched with new cloth, to receive new wine, we must love the Word of God more than our theologies and traditions.

Desire for God's Approval

Jesus was direct with the Pharisees: "How can you believe if you accept praise from one another, yet make no effort to obtain the praise that comes from the only God?" (John 5:44).

People with old wineskins often have a controlling and obsessive need to "accept praise from one another." Above all, they need the approval of the people around them.

This was certainly true of me. When I left my former church to help launch a Word-Spirit church, I cringed at the thought of how my friends and mentors would react to the news of my "defection." I chafed at the prospect of being labeled "charismatic." I wrote them a lengthy letter of explanation. I desperately wanted everyone to understand and endorse my new path.

Most wished me well, but a few disapproved. I should have anticipated the skepticism and criticism. After all, I had responded to others in the same way.

When God restores missing pieces, there is a consistent historical pattern. Those who receive the new pieces with open hearts and minds are opposed, often vehemently, by those most committed to the religion of the day. When Jesus and His disciples restored mercy to sinners, they were vilified by the Pharisees, the established religious experts of their time. When Luther restored the authority of the Bible and the concept of salvation by faith, the church excommunicated him and his followers. When the Anabaptists restored the notion of personal conversion and believers' baptism, early reformers mercilessly persecuted them. When George Whitefield and John Wesley restored the idea of preaching to the unchurched, the "most-churched" ostracized them. When William Carey restored the call to missions, he was scorned and rejected by his own pastors and elders. When modern pioneers restored private Bible reading and prayer, personal evangelism and follow-up, home Bible studies and lay ministry, contemporary music and evangelistic film, they were severely criticized and vehemently opposed by the religiously devout.

Part of embracing newly restored life with God is weathering the disapproval of others, including our spiritual families, friends, and mentors who matter most. To accept new wine, our hearts must genuinely and deeply desire the approval of God above the acceptance of people.

The Long Journey

It took me years and a number of spills to adopt these attitudes – and I'm still working on most of them. To let go of my old wineskin and adopt a new one, I had to overcome my own loyalties to the people and ideas that had formed my spiritual puzzle up to that point. I had to get past my doubts and personal aversion to risk. I had to come to a place where my hunger for God's presence and approval was greater than my desire for control, popular interpretations of His Word, and others' acceptance.

My journey was long and often difficult, and I would venture that shedding your old wineskin will not come easily for you either. You will doubt at times, and you will make mistakes. But no matter how tempted you are to give up, remember that God will never give up on you. He will continue to follow you, offering you the pieces you need to complete your spiritual picture. Even Peter, who denied his Lord three times when put to the test, recovered from that seemingly fatal misstep to become one of God's greatest servants and the foundation of His church. His failure was one of the final steps that allowed him to accept the Lord's new wine.

Are you fully awake? Are you ready to adopt a new wineskin? This is the moment when God can pour His new wine into your life — when you can begin receiving the vital missing pieces of your spiritual picture. It's time to take a deep breath and let God go to work.

For me, it began with two good friends and a troubled woman named Rose.

CHAPTER 7

NEW TERRITORY

Although she was in deep trouble, Rose was in the right place. She was in John and Jan Bingaman's living room. And if you were in trouble and needed spiritual help in Oklahoma City, the Bingamans' living room was the place to be. These two close friends, members of my congregation at Covenant Community Church, represented the most potent combination of wisdom, compassion, stamina, and relational capacity I have seen in my fifty years of Christian living.

After sitting down, Rose haltingly told her story. She had welcomed Jesus into her heart in college and lived a zealously devoted Christian life through her student years. After graduation, she moved to the West Coast to work with a Christian ministry. But when that opportunity dried up, she went into the business world.

As an executive recruiter, a headhunter, her success was dramatic. But so were the temptations. Before she realized what was happening, Rose found herself engulfed in Southern California's wild party scene. In the early 1980s, cocaine was the drug of choice; alcohol also flowed freely, and sexual immorality of all types was rampant. Rose indulged in everything that lifestyle had to offer for six years.

"Sometimes," rose told the Bingamans, "I wake up and it seems as if the real me has been abducted and locked away inside a deep, dark dungeon."

Rose recalled the goodness of her former life with God. It was so different then — more peace, more joy, more sense of direction. What had happened to her? If something didn't change, she would only become more miserable. She realized that she was on a roller coaster ride to ruin.

Before the day was over, Rose made the decision. It was time to return "home." Rose left her recruiting job, moved to Oklahoma City, and asked John and Jan to lead her through a rebuilding process. But Rose had a long way to go. Those years in California had taken an incredible toll on this once vibrant believer in Jesus. How would she get out of her dark prison of bondage?

John and Jan did what they knew to do, and it revolved around the Word. They helped Rose establish a daily quiet time for prayer and Bible reading. They insisted on serious weekly Bible study with other women at the church. They provided memory verses to renew her mind. They took Rose to the best available Christian counselor. They even moved her into their home for stretches of time, took her on vacations, and invited her to help with their ministry to others. She soon became an "adopted" member of the Bingaman family and a central part of women's ministry at Covenant Community Church.

Rose threw herself wholeheartedly into everything John and Jan suggested. And outwardly, things began to change. But inwardly, the pull to darkness was overwhelming.

"I would be finishing up my time in the Word, and it would seem as if something or someone was lurking, smirking, and mocking me," Rose would say. "I would have really good days when it seemed as though I was beginning to feel and breathe freedom, and then the next day I would be devastated by the power of darkness. It was a constant battle."

Even after months of determined effort, Rose was still locked behind invisible bars. The Bingamans were exhausted and frustrated. These were experienced servants of God. John had been discipled by a Navigator-trained friend. He was on the board of numerous citywide ministries, was an elder at our church, and acted as a spiritual father to dozens of young men. Jan had been a discussion leader and children's director for Bible Study Fellowship and had discipled dozens of young mothers in the community. Her gifts had attracted the attention of

Kay Arthur, who asked Jan to be a traveling trainer for Precept Ministries nationwide. In the past, John and Jan had enjoyed great success in leading others to a closer relationship with the Lord. But this time they were stymied. Their experience as Word people wasn't enough. For the first time, they found a gap in their spiritual jigsaw puzzle. Something was missing.

Fortunately, the Bingamans were not so locked into their traditions that they refused to bend or look for fresh solutions. They were willing to do whatever it took to help Rose.

They were ready for some new wine.

John and Jan prayed to God for an answer. They also began to ask around. "Is there anyone, anywhere, who is having success with people like Rose?" they would ask themselves, "Is there anything out there more effective than the approach we've been trying?"

Strange and Wonderful Things

As He always does, God responded to the Bingamans' sincere seeking. Within one memorable week, three unrelated people suggested that John and Jan check out an upcoming conference. These friends cautioned that they had never been to anything like this conference and were certainly not inclined to go themselves. But they'd read of strange things happening out there — wonderful things, if the reports were to be believed. People like Rose were being helped in dramatic ways.

The conference was on spiritual warfare. It would be held at the Anaheim Vineyard, a two thousand-member church that met in a former Wal-Mart building. It was located, of all places, in Southern California.

Desperate for a solution and believing that God was behind these urgings, John and Jan flew to Anaheim and sat in the back row for an evening service. It was different from anything they'd experienced before. The preacher sat on a stool on a makeshift stage. The worship time was loud and long. The congregation was dressed in everything from business suits to shorts and T-shirts. Yet their response to the service felt enthusiastic and genuine.

Even more amazing to John and Jan, however, was the story of the two young women who sat next to them that night at the conference. Several years earlier, both had been ministered to by teams of believers at the Anaheim Vineyard. According to the women, these teams had prayed, listened to the Spirit, sensed the influence of supernatural evil, and used the name of Jesus to confront and expel tormenting spirits.

In the months following the healing prayer, the Vineyard believers taught the women about the Father's love and introduced them to heartfelt worship. They taught about the presence, power, and ministry of the Holy Spirit. They encouraged the women to join a small house church, where the women studied Scripture, practiced spiritual gifts, and prayed for others.

The two women learned how to use their spiritual weapons to stay free and defend themselves from future torment. And they were free— outside and inside— from the compulsive desires that had previously dominated their lives.

It turned out that one of the women had become director of ministry training at the Anaheim Vineyard. Over the next few days of the conference, she tutored John and Jan on the ability to hear God, healing prayer, and deliverance. Then she loaded them with books and sent them back to Rose.

When Kingdoms Collide

When the Bingamans landed at the airport in Oklahoma City, Rose was there to meet them. The very next day, Jan put her hands on Rose's head and prayed, "Come, Holy Spirit."

Almost immediately, the forces of two kingdoms collided violently. Through- out the morning and afternoon, the battle raged. To Jan's surprise, as they worked their way through Rose's wounds and past sins, spirits within Rose surfaced in the form of guttural voices, convulsing fits of rage, and tirades of vulgar blasphemies. "I am going to hurt you! I am going to hurt her! You will never have her back — never!" The words came from Rose's mouth but sounded more like a mixture of growling and groaning.

Then Rose began crying. "Jan, I'm afraid. I'm scared. Will I be taken someplace where I can never come back?"

This was nothing like anything Jan had encountered before. But she pressed on. Through issue after painful issue, Rose alternated between clinging savagely to the past and repentant renunciation. Ever so slowly, Rose began to regain control over her soul.

By the end of the day, Jan and Rose were exhausted. For the first time, both had experienced a firsthand encounter with the invisible world. They had exercised spiritual gifts they had thought long extinct. They had heard God speak personally in ways they never imagined He would or could. They had felt the wrenching grip of supernatural evil and had seen it broken by the authority of Jesus' name. They had seen freedom, rest, and healing come into the life of a broken young woman.

Most important of all, both had *experienced* the love of God, the grace of Christ, and the powerful fellowship of the Spirit.

In the days that followed, John also joined in and saw firsthand the frightful clash of forces warring for Rose's body and soul. He found himself using prophetic messages that came through Jan and taking authority over the tormenting spirits. He witnessed demonic manifestations. He saw Rose strangely and wonderfully transformed as the grip of evil continued to be broken and the Father's love was revealed by the Spirit to Rose's inmost being.

This process deeply affected not just Rose but also John and Jan. It was significant even beyond Rose's deliverance from evil spirits and freedom from a sinful lifestyle. Through continuing visits to the Anaheim Vineyard with its extravagant worship, expectant and compassionate prayer teams, and bold use of spiritual authority and spiritual gifts, all three underwent an enormous paradigm shift. They experienced a radical change in the way they saw God and lived life with Him.

And it was only the beginning. Rose and the Bingamans were about to experience God even more in ways they'd never imagined. They would discover spiritual resources they never dreamed were available.

Without realizing it, they had broken through a wall into new territory — and they were about to pull me through with them.

"What Are You Going to Do?"

As John and Jan continued to work with Rose, they kept me abreast of their progress and frustrations. I felt a degree of powerlessness; I wasn't sure how to help, but I encouraged them to be open to new solutions God might reveal to them.

They had visited the Anaheim Vineyard without telling me beforehand. I think they feared my reaction to this radical step. But when they filled me in on what they learned there and the results it produced, I felt encouraged — as well as profoundly ignorant. This was out of my realm, yet it seemed to be making a difference. I felt a bit like Peter and his companions after the miraculous catch of fish. Before this, questions about the presence and power of God were safely "out there." Now they were in my boat! Philosophical musing about what God could and might do was no longer an option. The wolf — or the Lord — was at my door, and I had to engage.

John and Jan had seen a part of the church they didn't even know existed. They had heard ideas they'd never considered. At the Anaheim Vineyard, they had seen people prophesy with apparent accuracy and impact; they had heard prayers for the sick that apparently resulted in healing; they had seen evil spirits exposed and expelled with apparent success; they had heard people use a prayer language and appear to connect with God at some deeper level.

And now, calling on the Spirit with these same methods, they were seeing results with Rose.

John and Jan had questions. And because I was their pastor, they expected me to answer them: Is this real? Is this safe? Is it good? Is it biblical? Why haven't we heard about this before? Why don't we do this in our church? Seeing everything that's happened with Rose and hearing what we've told you, what are you going to do about this?"

By nature, I am a phlegmatic, peacekeeping, golden-retriever type. I hate crisis and despise controversy. But I had already been pondering the concept of spiritual missing pieces and wondering, "Is there more to God's working and the ministry of the Spirit than what we are currently expecting and experiencing?" And now the Bingamans expected me to provide spiritual answers to their questions — and to mine.

God was nudging me gently but firmly toward a breakthrough. It was time for me to discover my missing pieces.

Reading Time

I began by focusing even more intently on the Bible. I was struck again by the frequency of God's dramatic interventions: the Spirit of God taking over Saul and causing him to strip off his robes and lie prostrate "all that day and night," (1 Samuel 19:23-24); a prophet, Agabus, receiving revelation from the Spirit and prophesying famine on the Roman world(Acts 11:27-28); Peter healing a lame man, causing the man to praise God and stir "wonder and amazement" among those who saw him (Acts 3:6-10).

It was there on almost every page of the Old and New Testaments — clear examples of God's promises and commands, along with descriptions of His working among people in ways that allowed them and others to see that He is real and present.

These were the very things John and Jan had heard about at the Anaheim Vineyard and had experienced in helping Rose. As I read the Bible, I had to conclude that what they had encountered was genuine, biblical spiritual life. What they had experienced were very real pieces — for us, *missing* pieces — of life with God.

My reading extended to several other books. I started with John Wimber's *Power Evangelism* and was stunned by some of the "power encounters" he relates. For example, Wimber tells the story of sitting across the aisle from a businessman on a plane and feeling the Spirit directing him to deliver a message to this man. The message included the fact that the man was having an affair, the name of the woman involved, and a warning to stop the affair or face death. Wimber describes his struggle over relaying such a difficult message and then shares the conversation that followed:

> We sat . . . in strained silence. He looked at me suspiciously for a moment, then asked, "Who told you that name?"
>
> "God told me," I blurted out . . .
>
> "*God* told you?" He almost shouted the question, he was so shocked by what I had said.
>
> "Yes," I answered, taking a deep breath. "He also told me to tell you . . . that unless you turn from this adulterous relationship, he is going to take your life." . . . .
>
> In a choked, desperate voice he asked me, "What should I do?"

At last I was back on familiar ground. I explained to him what it meant to repent and trust Christ and invited him to pray with me. With hands folded and head bowed, I began to lead him in a quiet prayer. "O God...."[1]

That was as far as I got. The conviction of sin that had built up inside him seemed virtually to explode. Bursting into tears, he cried out, "O God, I'm so sorry" and launched into the most heartrending repentance I had ever heard.

My reaction to such accounts was excited and conflicted. I thought, "This is wonderful! I have read about this sort of thing in the Bible for years. It makes perfect sense. I knew God did this among His people. Now here it is!"

At the same time, I was overrun with skepticism. In all my years, I had never experienced this personally. I had been warned not to expect God to respond this way. I thought, "Wait a minute. Did this really happen? It must be an embellishment. It seems impossible."

I was torn. Maybe you're feeling the same way now as you read this book.

I kept reading: Dr. John White's *When the Spirit Comes with Power*, a psychiatrist's personal investigation into the Spirit's work among believers in the early days of the Anaheim Vineyard; Charles Kraft's *Christianity with Power*, a description of an evangelical seminary professor's shift from an "expect little, experience little" worldview to an outlook that embraced a supernatural, powerfully present God; Rich Nathan and Ken Wilson's *Empowered Evangelicals*, an account of God's amazing work among our evangelical forefathers and a call for evangelicals and Pentecostals to combine their strengths.

Most of what I read made great sense. It matched what I'd been reading in the Bible for years and what I imagined life with God could and should be like. But it was still so new, so foreign to what I'd ever encountered personally or been taught. It was hard to grasp or consider real. Up until then, I'd never been "in the room" to see any of the things I was reading about.

But that was about to change.

Coming Home

It started with visits to a small weekly worship gathering. On Saturday nights, our little band of renegades — John and Jan Bingaman, Bev, and I— joined about fifty others for services that included singing, kneeling, raising hands, weeping, and even dancing. It was radically different from the choirs, robes, and hymnbooks we were used to. These worship times were openhearted, affectionate, and intimate.

It was during these evenings that I began to realize how difficult it was for me to express my feelings toward God or even to feel much of anything for Him. I spent most of my time with my hands in my pockets, feeling uneasy, wanting to leave, and hoping nobody I knew would see me.

On the occasional Sunday when I didn't preach, I slipped away to the Vineyard church that met in downtown Oklahoma City. There, for the first time, I saw a church body regularly pray for people as part of their worship service.

They started with what seemed to me a rather extended time of worship (at that time, anything more than two consecutive songs felt extended to me) and a simple biblical message about God's willingness to work "right now." Then they listened for God's direction, an idea that had never occurred to me.

This was followed by an awkward time of silence. *What are we waiting for?* I thought, checking my watch and squirming uneasily in my chair.

The pastors conferred. One announced, "We sense that this morning God wants us to pray for people with shoulder pain; for those struggling with bitterness toward past abusers, especially young men who have been abused; and for those who have been seriously considering suicide this past week."

They invited anyone dealing with those issues to come forward. Prayer teams gathered around them, laid their hands on them, and began to pray. Most of the prayer was quiet, simple, and direct: "Lord, we ask in the name of Jesus that You heal Michelle's shoulder. Have compassion on her, Lord. Touch her even now. Holy Spirit, release Your healing power."

Another prayed quietly using strange words neither he nor I understood. It was one of the mysterious languages often translated as "tongues" in the Bible (see 1 Corinthians 12:10 and 14:2 for examples).

For another person, there was deliverance prayer. This was a little more emphatic, punctuated with firm words to some invisible spirit: "In the authority of Jesus, we command you to release David right now. We cancel your assignment and forbid you from speaking or working here. Go! You must go now in Jesus' name."

And for still another, the prayer sounded like this: "Lord, please come and speak to Steve. He is angry with his older brother who so brutally bullied him. He wants to forgive, but it's so hard. Would You come and say what You would say to help him?"

It was the strangest thing I'd seen in a church. People praying for healing, here and now, without a doctor — and *expecting something to happen*. People talking to evil spirits. People asking God to speak directly to His children.

I stood near these prayer teams listening in, wondering what, if anything, would happen, and hoping they wouldn't ask me to pray. I was a pastor, but to be honest, I wouldn't have known where to begin. I was used to receiving prayer requests and then, at a safe time later (assuming that I remembered), asking God to intervene. This "here and now" stuff was entirely new.

And then came our visit with the Bingamans to the conference in Kansas City in the summer of 1990. The exuberant worship. Bev and I raising hands. The healing of Josh Bingaman. The invigorating sense of discovery. And the indisputable challenge to my secure but less powerful spiritual upbringing.

God was moving me, pulling me across my self-imposed boundary to a place I never expected to go. But it was where I needed to be if I was to accept the missing pieces He was offering me.

He was telling me that the nagging questions in the back of my mind about the power and presence of the Spirit were about something more than just imagined possibilities. It really is true: God is just as mighty, just as engaged, and just as likely to work in miraculous ways *today* as He was during biblical times.

I realized that there is tremendous value in my evangelical, Bible-based experience. It is the foundation of who I am and who God will always be. It is the truth. Yet it is only part of the puzzle. My missing pieces were the power and ministry of the Holy Spirit. Only when I combined the truth of the Word with the experience of the Spirit would my picture be complete. Only then would I fully know, worship, and love the God who had created me.

It was the only explanation. And I was startled to realize that after all the years of wondering and searching, I actually believed it. My mind accepted it. My heart embraced it.

I was thrilled beyond description. And I was both a little scared and a lot relieved. I didn't realize it at the time, but I had inadvertently broken through a high, thick wall — a wall that had separated two sides of the church for one hundred years. What I did understand was that I felt closer to God than I ever had before.

I had just recovered a huge missing piece of spiritual life.

CHAPTER 8

THE WALL IS COMING DOWN!

I hope you are as excited as I am about the incredible significance of this discovery — that the joining of Word and Spirit is the key to fully experiencing God. But I realize that the story of my journey still may not be enough to convince you.

You may be thinking, *Sure, that seems to work for you, but what about me? What about other believers? It sounds good, but is anyone else buying into this crazy idea?*

The answer is yes; other believers today are seeing the value of a Word-Spirit experience. Millions of them.

According to researcher David Barrett, more than 50 million believers in the United States and 295 million worldwide have become part of a "mainstream [evangelical] church renewal" since 1980.[1] These are people outside Pentecostal denominations and beyond the charismatic movement. The Word neighborhood is in the midst of a Spirit revolution.

We see the impact of this revolution in almost every thriving evangelical church in America. Beginning slowly about 1975 and rapidly accelerating in the years since, the Word side of the church has undergone a dramatic increase in impassioned worship, healing prayer, attention to spiritual warfare, spiritual gifts, prayer and fasting, hope for revival, and intercession for an outpouring of the Spirit.

At the same time, we've seen a proliferation of Bible reading, Bible preaching, Bible teaching, and Bible study groups among Spirit people. Men such as Dr. Jack Hayford (Pentecostal Foursquare pastor and denominational head), Jack Taylor ("renewed" Southern Baptist pastor and revivalist) and Mike Bickle (International House of Prayer director) have become favorite speakers and authors for believers from all backgrounds. Christian bookstores now stock a variety of Bible study series and excellent study Bibles specifically written to strengthen Spirit-filled believers in their knowledge of the Scriptures.

Charismatics are becoming more evangelical in their hunger for Scripture and sound theology. Evangelicals are becoming more charismatic in their worship, prayer, and passion.

Why is this happening? It is because there is a wedding in progress. God is reconnecting the two halves of His church body. He is taking the best from the Word neighborhood and the best from the Spirit neighborhood to create a new kind of church—and a new kind of believer.

We are seeing the God-ordained wedding of Word and Spirit.

Our Word-Spirit Heritage

The romance leading up to this wedding has been a long one. Our evangelical past is actually filled with people who expected, encountered, and embraced vivid supernatural experiences as a regular part of life with God. As evangelicals, most of our renowned forefathers were Word-Spirit people, and they taught their followers to be the same. Some of our best-known Word-Spirit ancestors include the following people:

- *Reformer Martin Luther.* He openly waged spiritual warfare against the Devil and demons as he regularly sensed opposition. He saw the Holy Spirit and His gifts as a vital part of life with God.

- *Pietist and pioneer missionary Nicholas Von Zinzendorf.* He was part of the Moravian community that openly embraced direct revelations, signs and wonders, tangible outpourings of the Spirit, and inner personal awakenings to God's love.

- *Puritan theologians John Owen and Jonathan Edwards.* Owen authored the 651-page *A Discourse Concerning the Holy Spirit*, still the most extensive theological work on the subject. Edwards preached in a monotone, but he often observed dramatic effects on his listeners, including shrieking, wailing, shaking, and falling — all of which he acknowledged as genuine works of the Spirit.

- *Methodist founder John Wesley.* Wesley's journals, and the journals of those who traveled with him, are filled with references to our need for the Spirit's power, deliverances from demonic torment, and visible outpourings of the Spirit on his audiences. His theology of a second blessing that gives new power for holy living and influential ministry led to the later Pentecostal and charismatic teaching on the need for a "baptism of the Spirit."

- *Revivalist Charles Finney.* He also taught his listeners to seek and expect a tangible filling of the Spirit.

- *Evangelist D. L. Moody.* Best known for founding Moody Bible Institute, Moody also spoke adamantly about the importance of appropriating the ministry of the Spirit in a supernaturally empowering way.

- *Pioneer missionaries Hudson Taylor, Andrew Murray, and Amy Carmichael.* All three spoke openly about personal experiences with the Spirit and the need of His power for holy life and ministry.

The list could go on. Many of our highly respected evangelical ancestors enjoyed a vibrant relationship and life with the Spirit that reminds us of what's described in the New Testament and goes far beyond what most of us have been taught.

So what happened? Why have so many of us born and raised in good Bible-teaching churches seen and heard so little about experiencing the power of the Holy Spirit? Where did our rich heritage of life with the Spirit go?

It disappeared behind a wall.

Ignorance and Suspicion

With the dawn of the twentieth century came the Azusa Street revival in Los Angeles, an eruption of enthusiasm for the Holy Spirit, for the baptism of the Spirit, and for the gift of tongues. This revival turned interest in the power of the Spirit into a worldwide movement.[2] With it, however, came the inevitable errors, excesses, and improprieties common to spiritual awakenings. Rumors flew about this Holy Spirit "nonsense." Concerns mounted. Fears multiplied.

To protect their people and restore peace, denominational leaders of the early 1900s scrambled to rein in this new movement. Healing prayer, personal revelation, miraculous gifts, driving out demons, and outpourings of the Spirit were labeled "Pentecostal." The label was usually pronounced with contempt.

The wall went up.

Pentecostals were fenced out of mainstream denominations and became a denomination of their own. Although Pentecostalism shared the same fundamental beliefs as the evangelical tradition, it was marked by four distinct emphases:

- *Baptism in the Spirit.* Viewed as a dramatic post-conversion filling by the Spirit — a "second work of grace"; received by "tarrying" in earnest repentance, obedience, and prayer; seen as essential to empowered living and ministry; and confirmed by speaking in tongues.

- *Speaking in tongues.* Viewed as the supernatural gift of unlearned languages — human or angelic; intended for all believers; central to personal and corporate worship; and the universal sign of baptism in the Spirit.

- *Physical healing.* Taught as available "in the atonement" through the death and resurrection of Christ to all who would ask and believe.

- *Casting out demons.* Seen as an important part of Christ's Great Comission, the believer's authority, and the church's ministry to the world.[3]

Many evangelicals devoted to the Bible responded to the Pentecostal revival by teaching cessationism, the idea that the powerful miracles and miraculous gifts described in the New Testament were given only to Jesus, the apostles, and a few others to authenticate the gospel message and that these "signs and wonders" ceased with their deaths and the completion of New Testament writing.

Twentieth-century Word people still prayed, of course, but they tended to limit their requests to things God could do by sovereignly controlling natural process. They asked for healing through wise doctors and careful nurses, employment through favorable interviews, the election of desired candidates by leading the majority to vote for them, the soothing of emotional wounds through wise counsel and biblical instruction, needed funds through faithful givers, and friends being led to Christ through effective evangelists.

Cessationist-believing Word leaders extended this attitude to other means of experiencing God. They limited spiritual gifts to those that represented enhanced natural abilities (such as evangelism, teaching, and administration). They limited God's speaking to the Bible. They redefined prophecy as "forthtelling," commonly equated with preaching. They limited the authority of Jesus' name to the assurance of answered prayer. They limited the ministry of the Spirit to mental illumination, emotional comfort, and moral strengthening.

In other words, they erected a wall to keep the Spirit people with their supernatural expectations out. And as the years went by, both sides built on to the wall, adding height and depth. When a second Spirit awakening, the modern charismatic movement, emerged in 1960, conservative evangelicals responded by branding the movement as "charismatic chaos."[4]

Many on the Word side of the wall simply ignored their Spirit counterparts or dismissed them with derogatory stereotypes. Evangelicals often viewed the charismatic movement as the basement of our spiritual house. It contained some childish toys and little else. Spirit people were seen as intellectually care- less, emotionally unstable, a bit superstitious, and naïve in their outlook on life. While well intentioned, they didn't really understand what life and God are all about.

The view from the other side of the wall wasn't much better. To many Spirit people, the Word neighborhood was full of Ezekiel's dry bones. It was cold, dead orthodoxy. The people were heads without hearts, puffed up with knowledge, consumed with self-help, and built on self-effort. The Word side was seen as a place full of principles but lacking passion and power.

For nearly a century, many believers on both sides of the wall allowed ignorance and suspicion to shape their opinions of their spiritual brethren. Many today still hold to these views. They've been invited to the wedding, but they prefer the comfortable familiarity of where they are.

They don't know what they're missing.

Fuel and Fire

In many ways, those who cling to their Word-based or Spirit-based backgrounds are like bonfires not yet lit. In the case of evangelicals, all our discipline and knowledge is like a cord of wood stacked neat and high. We represent enormous potential energy. Yet what is astounding about us evangelicals, individually and corporately, is how small our impact has been for how much we know and how many we are. We have the *fuel* — the well-mastered truth about God — piled high in millions of lives. Yet something is missing.

Charismatics are also like one component of a potential bonfire. Their passionate power is a blazing torch. They represent incredible kinetic energy. But what is amazing about charismatics, individually and corporately, is how small their impact has been for how much they have and how many they are. They have the *fire* — the impassioned power of the fullness of the Spirit. Yet they too are missing something.

What both sides need is each other. Think of the bonfire that would burn in our churches, our denominations, our missions, and our own hearts if ever the often-quenched fire of the Holy Spirit was allowed to ignite the well-stacked fuel of biblical truth. We would feel the heat of an unprecedented blaze of spiritual fire and light! We would experience the message of the New Testament confirmed by the wonder-working power of the Spirit. We would be overwhelmed by a truth- power explosion that would consume the world in a life-giving way.

For too long, the torch burning on one side of the high, thick wall has been safely separated from the wood stacked on the other side. It's time for the wall to come down — for torch and fuel to ignite!

The Wall Crumbles

The Berlin Wall dividing West Berlin from East Germany was a symbol of the Cold War for nearly thirty years. During that time, more than eighty people died trying to cross over the wall into West Berlin. But on November 9, 1989, as the East German government teetered on collapse, a spokesman announced that the Berlin Wall was open. Thousands of overjoyed citizens raced to the wall to see for themselves. In enthusiastic rallies over the next week, they tore down large sections of the wall with sledgehammers, ropes, and even their bare hands.[5]

Many believers today are celebrating the collapse of another formidable barrier. God Himself is shaking the wall that has long separated Bible lovers from Spirit lovers. Whole sections are crumbling, leaving yawning gaps. Through these breaches, thousands of believers are flooding in both directions.

As they climb over the rubble, many are discovering the other half of their spiritual city, a half some never knew existed. They are finding that those who love the Bible are not coldhearted, intellectual elitists but are passionately devoted to Christ, dedicated to His Great Commission, full of wisdom, and rich in character. Others are realizing that those who love the Spirit are not emotionally unstable or weaker brethren plagued with shallow minds, inventive imaginations, and gullible souls. Instead, they have keenly discerning spirits, a biblical faith, and a deeply appealing boldness in life and ministry that is very much in touch with the present working of God.

Paul Stanley, for years an executive vice president on the Navigators International Leadership Team, traveled the world as part of his ministry. Several years ago I asked him, "Have you seen anything happening so extensively and increasing so dramatically that you sense it is a worldwide work of God?"

Without hesitating, Paul answered, "Oh, yes. There are four things that are happening *everywhere*." He went on to describe exactly what he'd observed:

- *An intense desire for worship.* "We used to be able to get by with a song or two to gather people before getting down to the real business of teaching and training. We can't do that anymore. People want to sing. They want to sing for thirty minutes to an hour. There is a broad, deep hunger for worship."

- *A strong movement toward prayer and fasting.* "It's not uncommon for me to get off an all-day flight and be pulled into an all-night prayer meeting. People want to pray and are willing to fast. There's a new awareness that life is supernatural, that we oppose evil supernatural powers, and that nothing short of prayer and fasting will defeat these powers and allow the gospel to progress."

- *A new zeal for evangelism.* "We don't see much of this in the West, but in developing countries there is a surge of passion to reach those who have never heard of Christ. Missionaries are regularly going from Ukraine to Siberia, from Korea to Nigeria, from Bulgaria to France, from Egypt to Iraq. There is a renewed awakening to the fact that the central work of God is seeking and saving those who are lost."

- *An expectant desire to see God manifest His power.* "People are no longer content to only read about the mighty works of God in the past or even to anticipate their return with Christ in the future. They are realizing that the Bible promises God's presence and power here and now. They want to experience God here and now. And they are seeing the power of God released as they ask Him to work."[6]

Paul Stanley is a Word man. His roots are Conservative Baptist. He's a West Point graduate with a keen appreciation for reason, order, and reality — the principles and neatness of the Word neighborhood. He has spent most of his spiritual life with the Navigators, which is very much a Word ministry. Yet he is seeing and acknowledging that something powerful and spiritual is happening in our world, something inexplicable from a strictly evangelical point of view. God is inspiring a movement that is shaking our comfortable foundations. The evidence is all around us.

In our Churches

Have you noticed what's happening with worship? Heads are up. Hands (or at least palms) are raised. We have new music and new instruments. The sound is intimate and affectionate — and sometimes just plain loud!

But it's more than that. We're singing *to* God rather than *about* Him. Lyrics extol God's love and power. The expression is enthusiastic and passionate. And this is happening in the majority of growing Word churches.

Beyond worship, many Word congregations have begun to ask their elders to lay hands on the sick and pray for healing. Some have formed deliverance teams that use programs such as author Neil Anderson's "Steps to Freedom" to expose and expel demonic torment. Some have initiated prayer counseling that includes listening to what the Spirit might reveal, asking Jesus to speak directly, and praying for God to break through in a supernatural way.

In addition, new churches are forming and deliberately joining the strengths of Word and Spirit traditions. They evangelize like Baptists. They teach Scripture and train in theology like Presbyterians. They worship and pray like Pentecostals. They defy traditional labels, and just about all who attend feel partly at home and partly stretched beyond their comfort zones. Many of these churches are "transdenominational," with believers from a broad spectrum of backgrounds who have a distinct desire to see the traditional denominational walls come down. These churches can be found in nearly every American city today.

One of these is Two Rivers Church, an Evangelical Free congregation in Knoxville, Tennessee. The church now numbers about 2,000 and provides a compelling example of what happens when people from a strong Word tradition embrace the power of the Spirit.

Here is a description of the Word-Power fusion that produced this new brand of vigorous church.

> A Word and power church is a community of God's people marked by the presence of the Spirit. It is a church that is rooted in the scriptures and alive in the power of the Spirit. I use the term "Word" to describe the Reformation stream of spirituality we've come to know in evangelicalism. I use the term "power" to describe the Pentecostal/charismatic stream of spirituality. These two streams of spirituality are merging together today in churches that don't want either the Word or the Spirit, but both the Word and the Spirit. Actually, I believe a Word and power church is really just a New Testament church
>
> The walls have nearly crumbled already in many parts of the world. The younger generation doesn't even realize there are walls. I have been invited to speak to Pentecostals about becoming more Word oriented and evangelicals about becoming more Spirit oriented. God is bringing together his people.[7]

Among Our Leaders

Listen to your pastors, especially the young ones. Notice their references to subjects such as healing prayer, spiritual warfare, the Holy Spirit, the Father's love, the importance of heart, the place of spiritual affection, and the value of freedom in worship.

Take note also of your pastors' involvement in prayer movements and citywide prayer summits. Peek in on those events, and you'll discover a rich mix of evangelical and charismatic men and women learning from each other.

Browse the books on your pastors' shelves. You may find titles that speak directly and boldly about the manifest presence of God, the ministry of the Spirit, and the importance of passionate worship.

If you ever have the opportunity, read the e-mails your pastors receive from church leadership networks. You'll find a loud, persistent call to move beyond speaking about God to allowing Him to work in powerful, visible ways. These messages have come from long-respected evangelical leaders such as George Barna and Richard Foster.

In more recent years this same call has been coming from such voices as Matt Chandler (Village Church), Sam Storms (Bridgeway Church), Jimmy Seibert (Antioch Ministries International), and Francis Chan (We Are Church).

This isn't to say that either your pastors or these leaders embrace the particulars of Pentecostal theology or the excesses of the charismatic movement. They don't. But they are calling evangelicals to rediscover significant ministries of the Spirit that are thoroughly biblical and have been largely confined to the other side of the Word-Spirit wall.

In Our Publications

It began as a trickle with Billy Graham's 1978 book *The Holy Spirit*. It gained momentum through the contributions of Campus Crusade's Bill Bright. Today, with the addition of many new writers, we are seeing a flood of books on the Spirit, revival, experiencing God, hearing God's voice, spiritual warfare, impassioned worship, and intercessory prayer.

Many of these writers are known and respected Word scholars and pastors.

Some of their titles from recent years include the following:

- *Forgotten God: Reversing our Tragic Neglect of the Holy Spirit* by Francis Chan

- *Spirit and Sacrament* by Andrew Wilson.

- *Hearing God* by Dallas Willard

- *Surprised by the Power of the Spirit* and *Surprised by the Voice of God* by Jack Deere

- *Convergence: Confessions of a Charismatic Calvinist* by Sam Storms

- *Prayer* and *Streams of Living Water* by Richard Foster

- *Kingdom Triangle* by J. P. Moreland

- *Wild at Heart* and *Waking the Dead* by John Eldredge

- *Windows of the Soul* by Ken Gire

- *Experiencing God* by Henry Blackaby

Consider the following excerpt from Chuck Swindoll's book *Flying Closer to the Flame*. As a past president of Dallas Theological Seminary, Chuck Swindoll is the epitome of a Word leader, yet he writes forcefully about recovering our neglected relationship with the Holy Spirit:

> Since the Spirit of God was sent not only to be studied but ultimately to be experienced, it seems to me we have stopped short of God's intended purposes when we merely discuss and debate His presence instead of exulting in Him on an intimate basis. Long enough have non-charismatic, evangelical Chris-

tians (I am both) stood at a distance, frowning and throwing spiritual stones at those in God's family who did not dot every "i" or cross every "t" exactly the same as we. . . .

During my growing up years, including my years in seminary, I kept a safe distance. I was taught to be careful, to study Him (the Holy Spirit) from a doctrinal distance but not to enter into any of the realms of His supernatural workings or to tolerate the possibility of such. Explaining the Spirit was acceptable and encouraged; experiencing Him was neither. Today, I regret that. I've lived long enough and ministered broadly enough to realize that flying closer to the flame is not only possible, it is precisely what God wants.[8]

Consider also this excerpt from Francis Chan's *Forgotten God.* It is particularly significant in light of Chan's roots, training, and ministry in the part of the evangelical church that has been regularly and rigorously opposed to the idea of New Testament-like power of the Holy Spirit for today.

> You might think that calling the Holy Spirit the "forgotten God" is a bit extreme. Maybe you agree that the church has focused too much attention elsewhere but feel it is an exaggeration to say we have forgotten about the Spirit. I don't think so.
>
> From my perspective, the Holy Spirit is tragically neglected and, for all practical purposes, forgotten. While no evangelical would deny His existence, I'm willing to bet there are millions of churchgoers across America who cannot confidently say they have experienced His presence or action in their lives over the past year. And many of them do not believe they can....
>
> There's more of the Spirit and more of God than any of us is experiencing. I want to go there – not just intellectually, but in life, with everything that I am.[9]

Finally, consider the older, long-respected voice of Dallas Willard – again, significant because of his evangelical roots, his extensive knowledge of the scriptures and his incisive thinking. He says this about the importance of hearing God in a direct, personal, experiential way.

> Hearing God? A daring idea, some would say – presumptuous and even dangerous. But what if we are made for it? What if the human system simply will not function properly without it? There are good reasons to think it will not. The fine texture as well as the grand movements of life show the need. Is it not, in fact, more presumptuous and dangerous to undertake human existence *without* hearing God?[10]

This paradigm shift in thinking is reflected not only in evangelical publications. During the same period of time, there has been a dramatic increase in study Bibles, Bible dictionaries, and Bible study materials written for Spirit people by their scholars and pastors. For example, *The New Spirit-Filled Life Bible*, edited by Jack Hayford, is an outstanding Word-Spirit study text. Similarly, Pentecostal scholar Dr. Gordon Fee is the author of *God's Empowering Presence: The Holy Spirit in the Letters of Paul* and *Paul, The Spirit and the People of God* — both widely praised by evangelical scholars for their exegetical excellence.

In Mission Reports

In chapter 5, we examined mission reports springing from the showing of Campus Crusade's *JESUS* film. They are just a few of the many amazing stories coming in from around the world. Here is one more example from Jerry White, former international president of the Navigators:

> An African believer wanted to tell a young man about Jesus. The young man, a committed Muslim, refused to listen, saying, "If Jesus is who He said He is, He needs to reveal Himself personally to me." The believer asked if he could at least pray aloud for him, and the young man agreed to that. Some years later,

the young Muslim man saw an unusual light shining through his window. A form appeared, identified Himself as Jesus, and referred to the prayer that was prayed over him years before by the believer. The Muslim man did not go to prayers at the mosque that day, and everyone wondered where he was. Later he went to the mosque and told how he had become a believer in Jesus. His friends were furious, took him outside, beat him, and left him to die. A Christian family found him, took him to a safe place, and nursed him back to health. . . .[11]

I was encouraged to hear story after story about God's amazing grace in Africa. Please pray that our staff will experience God's power and creativity in bringing Africa into the Kingdom.

What we have here is a prominent Christian Word leader openly reporting on the supernatural power of God — and asking others to pray that his staff will experience more of it.

At Nationwide Rallies

Increasingly, wherever God gathers large groups of His people - one thousand or one hundred thousand; men, women, or youth - He now mixes a potent blend of people from both Word and Spirit neighborhoods. As early as the 1990s, Promise Keepers speakers (such as Chuck Swindoll and Jack Hayford) and worship leaders (such as the Maranatha Singers and Vineyard worship teams) hailed from each side. If you visit a Navigator, Campus Crusade, or Inter-Varsity event, you will find youth from all backgrounds worshiping passionately, praying for healing, interceding for revival, and calling for an outpouring of the Spirit.

Wherever God gathers His people, the wall is now coming down.

That First Step

As Word people and Spirit people, we represent two enormous groups who share the same Savior, the same Scriptures, the same desire for holiness, and the same hope for eternity. Yet for too many years we've barely acknowledged that the other side exists. We've known little of the essential truths, resources, and processes that have been discovered and preserved in the other neighborhood. We've missed out on the significant spiritual pieces available on the other side of the wall.

But that wall is coming down! Just as the Berlin Wall cracked and crumbled, the Word-Spirit barricade is falling to pieces. People are moving through the gaps. Many evangelicals are discovering Spirit torches and are returning to ignite holy bonfires at home.

You too may be standing at the base of this crumbling spiritual wall, peeking over the rubble, ready to risk stepping through and accepting the power promised there. You want to know more. You see others finding answers. And you desperately want to complete the spiritual picture of your life and fully experience God.

Cautiously, you lift your foot over the scattered bricks and concrete. You step forward. You've done it! You're on the other side!

So what happens now?

CHAPTER 9

COMPLETING THE PICTURE

If you've taken that fateful first step over the wall and are now standing on the other side, ready to explore a strange new world, give yourself a pat on the back. You've come a long way just to arrive at this spot.

A step over the wall means that you've already been through a process of awakening. It may have included digging deeper into God's Word, noticing and acknowledging what is happening spiritually around the world, taking stock of your personal encounters with members of that other neighborhood, or simply listening more closely to God's gentle whispers to your heart. It may have been a combination of all of these mixed with fervent prayer that God's will for your life would be revealed. It may even be that this book was the final nudge you needed to move forward.

In addition, your awakening has surely involved a shift in attitude. As you've sensed that you're missing something spiritually, something vital that God longs to give you, you've likely become more humble, more hungry for His presence, more willing to hear and adopt whatever He is about to tell you.

As you stand here on the border of a new frontier, excited and perhaps a bit apprehensive, be encouraged. God has walked with you throughout your journey, guiding you patiently to this very place. He's not going to abandon you now.

Though I have written this book primarily for those with an evangelical background, it's possible that you come to this point in the book — and in your life — from a mostly charismatic experience. If that is so, I urge you to look for the four great strengths in the Word neighborhood. Your travels here will be far more rewarding if you consider the rich value of each:

- *The discipline of study.* Repeatedly, the Bible commands us to meditate on God's Word. When combined with the right spirit, conscientious study of Scripture does not produce coldhearted spiritual eggheads. Instead, it yields "a workman who does not need to be ashamed and who correctly handles the word of truth" (2 Timothy 2:15).

- *The value of knowledge.* While it is true that knowledge with an arrogant heart "puffs up" (1 Corinthians 8:1), it is also true that "through knowledge the righteous escape" (Proverbs 11:9). We can neither trust nor obey truth we don't know.

- *The limitations of faith.* Biblical faith submits to the inscrutable will of God. It recognizes that no matter how strong our faith is, there will be many no's for reasons only God knows. It recognizes that although we do indeed have awesome first fruits of the Spirit's power and authority, we will continue to groan in body and soul until the Rescuer returns to complete the job (see Romans 8:22-23).

- *The imperative of holiness.* Biblical worship combines both adoration and character. It's a call to "sing and make music in your heart to the Lord . . . [and] submit to one another out of reverence for Christ" (Ephesians 5:19,21). It also means to "lift up holy hands in prayer, without anger or disputing" (1 Timothy 2:8). Enthusiastic praise during worship without right living in everyday life is a grievous inconsistency.

On the other hand, you may have approached the Word-Spirit wall from the evangelical side and are now about to enter the neighborhood where charismatics reside. If so, you too will see here four great strengths God wants for us all.

- *The power of prayer.* On paper, we evangelicals have got it. Verbally, we affirm it. In practice, we neglect it. Paul said, "I urge, then, first of all, that requests, prayers, intercession and thanksgiving be made for everyone" (1 Timothy 2:1, emphasis added). We need to pray for people rather than talk them to death.

- *The priority of worship.* We Word people have exalted the mind and reviled the heart for too long. Life with God is a romance built on both faithfulness and affection. It is sustained by worship that is biblically free in both form and expression. Worship is as crucial to vibrant life with God as is daily Bible reading, regular evangelism, and faithful service. In fact, worship is the spring from which the rest flow.

- *The significance of spiritual gifts.* It is time to stop despising and prohibiting the study, pursuit, and exercise of the supernatural abilities the Spirit gives His people for ministry. It is time to stop slurring the relevant passages. It is time to stop replacing biblical instruction with traditions that are more comfortable and easier to manage. The moment has arrived to unlock the closet and allow our disciples to use these tools under the clear, straightforward direction of the New Testament.

- *The reality of supernatural warfare.* Satan lives, and so do his spirits who demonize saved and lost alike. His oppressive, crippling grip will be broken only as we deliver one another by the power of the Spirit and the authority of Jesus' name.

These road signs are much more than mile markers you barely notice as you speed past. They should not be ignored or dismissed. They are critical to the success of your journey. Think of them as "Point of Interest" signs that will guide you to the most fascinating and rewarding places in the neighborhood.

If you follow the arrows, you'll see and experience God in ways that will dramatically enrich your life with Him.

Rules for the Road

So here you are. The moment has come. It's time to explore what God has to tell you about this strange place on the other side of the wall.

How shall you proceed?

Let me offer you four rules for the road as you begin:

Rule 1: Step Out

Start by taking a day off from your usual Sunday church routine. Visit a congregation known for the presence of God, for prophecy, for a healing ministry, or for its enthusiastic worship. If you don't know where to begin, make your best guess. Most likely it will be a different denomination than what you're used to.

When you arrive, don't automatically choose the last seat in the back row of the building. You're here not just to observe but to participate! Try at least for a spot somewhere in the middle.

When the service begins, remember that things are going to be a little different. Let yourself be comfortable with being uncomfortable. Ask God to help you set aside your nervousness or wariness. Remember that He is with you every step of the way.

Before or after the service, seek out members of the congregation and ask them to share information about their church and their own spiritual story. Most people, if they sense that your interest is genuine, will be happy to respond. If your first visit isn't everything you'd hoped for, don't be discouraged. Give it another try or attend a different church.

It will take more than one attempt to discover everything God has in store for you.

In addition, talk to friends and watch the newspaper for notices about upcoming conferences. Attend one that combines Bible teaching with healing prayer, prophecy, and spiritual warfare. You may discover more similarities to your spiritual background than you expected. I recognize that it isn't easy to break out of your comfort zone, but I also believe that if you've come this far, you're ready for the next step.

I'm reminded of a woman named Kelly. As a girl, she'd attended church from time to time. But the teaching seemed lifeless to her, and she drifted away from God as she grew up.

Kelly was a young woman when I saw her one Sunday morning at Bridgeway Church in Oklahoma City. It had been many years since she had been inside a church. She'd come early and sat by herself in the back row with shoulders rounded forward, legs crossed, and head buried in the bulletin. I doubt she made much sense of what she read, but it was the best available place to hide from the awkwardness of a largely empty auditorium. I could tell she felt out of place.

When we were joined by the seven or eight hundred "regulars" who make up the Bridgeway congregation, I was surprised that this young woman remained. I imagine the bustle and happy chatter only increased her urge to run.

As the lights dimmed and we began to worship, Kelly must have felt some relief at the relative anonymity. Worship at Bridgeway is always a rich mix of celebration, affection, and devotion. Kelly could not have missed the people's enthusiasm and joyful wonder.

At the end of the worship time, the prophetic team stood to minister. These men and women had demonstrated a genuine ability to receive messages from God and to deliver them to others "for their strengthening, encouragement and comfort" (1 Corinthians 14:3). They all had the biblical gift of prophecy and the spiritual maturity to do it effectively.

The first person to speak was a middle-aged doctor's wife named Kathleen. "I have a message for you," she said into the microphone. She pointed to the far edge of the auditorium — right at Kelly.

She asked Kelly to stand. Slowly, her face red and her knees wobbling, Kelly made it to her feet.

"The Lord has shown me that he sees the heart you have to be a good mother," Kathleen said to Kelly. "He sees your love for your child. He sees your desire to provide the best. He sees the sacrifices you've made. He loves who you are and what you've been as a mother."

As Kathleen spoke, Kelly began to weep. Though I doubt she could have put her feelings into words, she was waking up to the reality that God knew her personally and loved her enough to pick her out of a crowd of people and speak directly to her.

Kathleen didn't know how on target her message was. Kelly was, in fact, a mother — a single mom. In many ways, she was a hard woman. But she was also a determined one. Her pride and joy was her six-year-old son. Day after difficult day she juggled the demands of putting herself through the local university, supporting herself and this child, and raising him so that he would not grow up to be like the father who had abandoned him.

Had you opened Kelly's heart that morning, you would have found lots of questions. From my conversations with her after that Sunday, I can assure you that two of her most pressing concerns were, "How will I ever make it?" and "Can I ever come back to God?"

That morning, He answered both.

What Kelly didn't realize was that she was experiencing the fusion of Word and Spirit. She was benefiting from what happens when we combine the best of the evangelical tradition with the best of the charismatic church.

You may not have a dramatic, personal encounter with God on your first journey to the other side — but then again, if He sees that you need it and are ready for it, you just might!

Rule 2: Expand Your Circle

When you are on a quest for your missing spiritual pieces, it's often hard to find people who understand what you're going through. Those closest to you may be uncomfortable with what you're doing and what's happening inside you. Yet if you're reading, thinking, praying, and experiencing this alone, it can be extremely lonely, and you can easily become discouraged.

This is a time to expand your circle. Connect with others, in your church or elsewhere, who are also discovering that something is missing. I know that John and Jan Bingaman appreciated being able to bounce questions and ideas off of Bev and me as we explored the Spirit neighborhood together— and we were grateful for them as well.

As Solomon wrote, "Two are better than one. If one falls down, his friend can help him up" (Ecclesiastes 4:9-10). So find a kindred spirit! Have coffee and open your heart.

Rule 3: Ask for Prayer

The apostle James spoke clearly:

> Is any one of you in trouble? He should pray. Is anyone of you sick? He should call the elders of the church to pray over him and anoint him with oil in the name of the Lord. And the

prayer offered in faith will make the sick person well; the Lord will raise him up. If he has sinned, he will be forgiven. Therefore confess your sins to each other and pray for each other so that you may be healed. The prayer of a righteous man is powerful and effective. (5:13-16)

This passage applies specifically to physical sickness as a manifestation of God's discipline for sin. Beneath the specifics, however, are a broader principle and application. When we sense that something is missing or broken or needs fixing, we ought to be humble enough to confess our need and ask another to pray for us. This applies to anytime in life when we are seeking to complete our spiritual puzzles.

When God hears this kind of humble prayer, His response is indeed often "powerful and effective." He breaks through in areas we cannot break through on our own.

Chad and Sandy experienced God's power after their son, Andrew, developed serious breathing difficulties when he was just three weeks old. Unless he was hooked up to bottled oxygen and machines that monitored his breathing, Andrew often "crashed" — he briefly stopped breathing, and his blood oxygen plunged to dangerously low levels. His doctors were baffled.

At the suggestion of a friend, Chad and Sandy had already taken their struggling baby son to a Pentecostal church in another town where an itinerant prayer healer was ministering. A member of the healer's prayer team there had prayed for Andrew. Nothing changed.

The next day the prayer healer was coming to Chad and Sandy's city. Their friend called again and told Chad and Sandy she had a strong sense that they should try again, this time with the prayer healer himself.

They were reluctant to go. After all, they were Word people. This was far out stuff. And they'd already tried once.

But they were desperate.

Chad, Sandy, and Andrew arrived late to the meeting — so late that the preaching and prayer time were already finished. The visiting preacher-healer was on his way out the door.

Embarrassed and frantic, they blocked the man's exit, Chad carrying the oxygen and monitors and Sandy holding Andrew. "Please, we've brought our sick boy," Chad said. "The doctors say they can do nothing. Would you please pray for him?"

The man stopped. He was exhausted. He had been on the road for days. The night's ministry had been long and draining. But when he heard that nothing could be done for little Andrew, he said, "We'll see about that."

He then prayed the simplest prayer for healing and walked out.

Sandy felt something eerie course through her body, like a pulse of electricity. Chad didn't know what to think. He just cried from the weariness of it all — and wondered.

When they got home, they took Andrew off his oxygen. They kept his monitors connected and watched and waited.

And watched and waited.

And watched and waited some more.

A day went by with no crashing.

Then another day. Then a week.

Finally Sandy called the medical supply company and told them to come get their machines and oxygen tanks. Incredibly, Andrew never crashed or needed the machines again.

If you long to see God work, I encourage you to find someone to hear your desire, lay hands on you, and ask God's Spirit to reveal what's missing, heal what's broken, impart gifts, or deliver a breakthrough. When it comes to laying on of hands, the biblical teaching is too foundational (see Hebrews 6:1-2) and the examples too numerous to ignore (see Jesus in the Gospels; …2 Tim 1:6).

Rule 4: Study the Word

As you continue your explorations of your new spiritual neighborhood, it will be more important than ever for you to stay grounded. I urge you to persist in studying and relying on the Word of God (if you're an evangelical, this may come as a welcome relief!).

God's presence, His spiritual gifts, His personal love for us, and His desire for our passionate worship are not novel ideas. They are foundational truths taught plainly throughout Scripture. But they've been caught by the filters of our culture, theology, and traditions. Your best response to whatever God is teaching you about missing pieces may be to reread His Word. As you do, watch for the appearance of your own missing pieces.

You may want to try what I did. I bought a four-color pen(two different colors are what you'll need) and read the Word, beginning with the New Testament and reading straight through. Wherever God did something supernatural, spoke personally, healed the sick, delivered the demon-possessed, sent an angel, or miraculously freed someone from danger, I underlined the passage in green.

Then I did the same throughout the Old Testament.

Give it a try. You'll discover that the green flows freely! From Genesis, when God spoke personally to Adam and Eve in the garden, to the closing chapter of Revelation, when Jesus appeared to John on the island of Patmos, God was present and taking supernatural action among His people. Remember Paul's instruction: "Now these things happened as examples for us." (1 Corinthians 10:6, NASB). God's work through the generations should not merely show us what He did thousands of years ago. It should, as He tells us directly, show us what we can expect to see Him do among us today.

Now change your pen to red and use it to trace the emotion in Scripture. Underline the moments of strong feelings, deep affections, intense joys, deep sorrows, rich affections, and extravagant worship. Your Bible will soon be filled with so much red and green that you'll be thinking about Christmas!

Notice the compassion of Abraham as he pleads for Sodom and Gomorrah (see Genesis 18:16-33), the excitement and determination of Jacob after his spiritual dream at Bethel (see Genesis 28:10-22), the uncontainable enthusiasm of David as he returns the ark to Jerusalem (see 2 Samuel 6), the clear call to impassioned worship in the Psalms (see Psalms 95–100; 145–150), and Paul's instruction to "make music in your heart to the Lord" (Ephesians 5:19).

Our God is an emotional God. He calls us to be emotional people. God longs for us to see the greatness of His passionate love for us and to reciprocate. If you keep this in mind and continue to rely on His foundation, you will benefit immeasurably during your travels on the other side of the wall.

Your Time Has Come

This is your moment. Reading, thinking, and analyzing are vital, but they will only take you so far. After reading about healing prayer, there comes a time to lay hands on the sick and pray for God to touch and heal. After hearing that God speaks directly, there comes a time to listen and to share what you sense He is saying to you. After reading about our authority over evil spirits, there comes a time to take that authority and speak to tormenting spirits in your life and in the lives of tormented friends. After reading about the psalmist's call to total, enthusiastic, and unashamed worship, there comes a time to raise your hands in awe and surrender, shout and clap in praise and thanksgiving, and dance for joy. The time has come — if you truly want to recover the missing pieces God is holding out to you — to stop analyzing other people's motives, stop fearing the potential problems, stop debating the theological merits, and stop watching others.

It's time to grab hold with both hands and start *doing* it.

When that happens, you'll have more than theories to discuss. You'll have stories to tell and testimonies to give. You will *experience* the power of the Holy Spirit. Before long, you will encounter the love and presence of God in specific and tangible ways. You will find yourself "in the room" as God works. And you will be able to bear witness not only to what you have heard but also to what you have seen and felt of the saving love and power of God.

You will not just read the New Testament; you'll live it. You will be able to say with the apostle John, "We proclaim to you what we have *seen and heard*, so that you also may have fellowship with us" (1 John 1:3, emphasis added).

You'll recover some large missing pieces.

CHAPTER 10

THE PURPOSE OF PASSION

In 1996, just months after I joined Bridgeway Church as a senior pastor, we decided to host a conference. Being a fledgling congregation of about two hundred members, the thought was a bit ridiculous. But the concept was exciting — an event designed to give evangelicals a safe place to explore and experience the wedding of Word and Spirit. We would offer affectionate worship, biblical teaching on the "missing pieces," prophetic ministry by those with proven gifting, and healing prayer for those willing to receive it.

I was comfortable with everything but the conference title. We called it "Passionate Love for Jesus." None of those words felt right to me.

Passionate seemed too worldly, too Hollywood, too sensuous, too romantic. If we were running a film festival showcasing R-rated romance, then maybe. But for an event featuring God and the Bible? I felt it didn't fit.

Love seemed too soft, too overused. If we used the words *full devotion* or *heart commitment* or *radical obedience*, I would have been content. But *love* just seemed too mushy.

Jesus. At least, I thought, let's include the title *Lord*. *Jesus* was too friendly, too familiar, too intimate.

The title as a whole seemed childish. It was too emotional and touchy-feely. I was almost embarrassed to connect my name and the name of Bridgeway Church to the cluster of images and ideas that arose from "Passionate Love for Jesus." Would a sound minded, level headed evangelical come to a conference with a name like that?

On the day of the event, to my surprise, I discovered that fourteen hundred of them would.

Resistance

If you are a Word person like me, you may encounter resistance as you delve further into the Spirit neighborhood. Not from God. Not from the Spirit people you come across. But from deep inside yourself.

During my first ventures into the Spirit church, I repeatedly struggled with the concept of letting loose spiritually. Remember my embarrassment in Kansas City when John Bingaman found me worshiping with hands raised at ear level? The experience was profoundly uncomfortable.

By the time I joined the staff at Bridgeway, I was obviously still struggling.

Why did I find the emotional side of life with God so difficult? Why the locking up? Why the involuntary sweating? Why the irrepressible embarrassment?

Part of it, I am sure was my upbringing in the home of a fighter-pilot father where staying cool was the ultimate value.

Another part, no doubt, was the think-don't-feel emphasis of my engineering training.

But looking back, I can see that the basis for my emotional restraint grew out of the culture of my Word neighborhood. With all the emphasis on living by the Book, not only were our spiritual minds deliberately accentuated, but our spiritual passions were deliberately repressed. And for what we saw as good reasons:

- *Emotionalism.* In a world of ups and downs, it was vitally important that our faith and devotion rest solidly on the promises of God's Word and not on emotional reactions. Certainly, feelings were a part of our relationship with God, but they were the least important part. They were the caboose on the train. Minimizing emotion stabilized spiritual life.

- *Order.* The Scriptures clearly state that in both personal life and public gathering, God calls us to do all things "in a fitting and orderly way." (1 Corinthians 14:40). Emotion made it easy for our thinking, speaking, and behavior to degenerate into disarray. The dangers multiplied in groups. Wise leaders helped people keep their feelings under a firm rein.

- *Reputation.* Christianity was already on shaky ground with thoughtful outsiders. Emotional displays with unbelievers present would only further their impression that faith is for the foolish and unstable. For the sake of God's reputation and that of the gospel, we needed to vigilantly preserve an appearance of reason and avoid anything that associated spirituality with instability.

- *Consideration.* When we gathered to worship, we often had visitors. These visitors, like the rest of us, might become extremely uncomfortable in the midst of emotional display. Even where feelings might be legitimate, the visitors might not understand either the reason or the intensity. In deference to these newcomers, an appearance of calm and emotional stability was crucial.

- *Immaturity.* As we all knew, releasing strong feelings was simply immature. That's why we were so uncomfortable with it, especially those of us who valued words, ideas, and truth. If we were to become people with clear minds, unmistakable objectives, and effective behavior — people who commanded the respect of others, inspired confidence, and persevered in difficulty — we had to keep our feelings in check. We simply could not afford to be ruled by passion.

These were all good reasons, good enough to make someone like me — raised in a no-cry family, trained as an engineer, comfortable with military demeanor — profoundly uneasy with intense passion. I simply didn't like it.

And yet....

The Biblical Call to Passion

Despite my sound reasoning and personal awkwardness with emotion, something deep inside me kept whispering that passion and God do, in fact, go well together. In spite of my strong preference for calm and control, I knew that the very nature of God, His majesty and wonder, requires a passionate response. It was Christ, after all, who said that "because you are lukewarm — neither hot nor cold — I am about to spit you out of my mouth" (Revelation 3:16).

Even though I felt most comfortable with the sedate style of worship in my own spiritual neighborhood, I couldn't help but sense that it was missing something when compared to the Bible. So I revisited the Scriptures, looking specifically for emotion.

I found plenty of it.

As I've already explained, our Lord is a God of emotion. He is capable of love (see Exodus 34:6-7; John 3:16), rage (see Numbers 11:1; John 2:14-16), jealousy (see Exodus 20:5), grief (see Genesis 6:6; Ephesians 4:30), joy (see Zephaniah 3:17; Luke 10:21), and much more. He expresses these feelings freely, and He fully expects us to express them as well.

To know and experience God is to know and experience passion.

I found this passion prominent in the Psalms. The Psalms are full of direct commands to God's people throughout the ages to feel deeply and express freely — and examples of what this looks like. Joy, grief, awe, confidence, and devotion are all experienced intensely and expressed extravagantly. Whether it be through shouting, clapping, dancing, weeping, kneeling, or raising hands — sometimes in praise, sometimes in honor, sometimes in desperate need — God openly calls each of us to passionate expression:

> *Shout for joy to the LORD, all the earth, burst into jubilant song with music;*
>
> *make music to the LORD with the harp, with the harp and the sound of singing,*
>
> *with trumpets and the blast of the ram's horn — shout for joy before the LORD, the King.*

(Psalm 98:4-6)

The Psalms, as well as many other places in Scripture, call us to *feel* life and to *express* it to each other and to God with open hearts. There is nothing staid about the biblical picture of life with God. When it comes to God and His goodness, there is nothing commendable about being calm and collected.

As you trace the expression of feeling through the Psalms, you cannot help but sense that emotion is crucial not only to *revealing* what is in our hearts but also to *shaping* our hearts. God commands us to shout our praises, sing for joy, weep over our sin, and vent our anger, confusion, doubt, and longing. Why?

Try it, and you'll find out. Not only do our minds influence our emotions (something we understand well in the intellectual West), but our emotions, when expressed, shape our minds. When we shout praises to God, literally lifting our faces and voices upward, we understand His magnificence at a deeper level. When we let ourselves groan and weep over our sin, we often realize the ugliness and damage of it, and we sense a surge of desire to get out and stay out. When we ask our painful questions, the Spirit often reveals comforting answers. When we cry out our sorrow, we experience a strange restoration of relief and hope.

This is why God calls us — no, *commands* us — to feel and to express. This is why it's vital that we respectably reserved evangelicals recover the missing piece of passion.

But that's not all. Emotional expression not only sharpens our minds, but it also communicates what we have in our life with God to those who might be visiting or looking in from the outside. We are better examples of the true nature of God when we allow our experience of Him to shine through. God wants His people to have full and open hearts, and He wants our godly passion to show through to all who might be looking on.

As I searched the Scriptures, I also found passion in the great stories of personal and corporate worship. In each case, the biblical author makes it clear that God loves what's going on. Think of the Israelites celebrating their rescue from Pharaoh (see Exodus 15:1-21), David dancing before the Lord (see 2 Samuel 6:16-23), Solomon dedicating the temple (see 1 Kings 8), Mary adoring Jesus at Bethany (see Luke 10:38-42), and the early church interceding for boldness in the face of persecution (see Acts 4:23-31).

In every one of these examples, we see God approving and responding positively to what's happening. More important to us evangelicals, it's clear that He wants us to notice, to remember, and to join in.

Even in the highly instructional letters of Paul, I found impassioned worship prominently displayed. Throughout his letters, Paul's carefully reasoned theology and application are regularly punctuated with unrestrained outbursts of praise, thanksgiving, and wonder (see Romans 11:33-36; 1 Corinthians 1:4-9; 2 Corinthians 1:3-7; Ephesians 1:3-14; and, most famously, Eph 3:14-21).

Whichever part of the Bible we examine, it is clear that God wants our life with Him to be passionate. He wants us to be *intellectually* passionate — in awe and eager to understand all He has revealed about Himself and His plans through His Word. We are to love Him with all of our minds. He desires us to be *devotedly* passionate — willing to obey, ready to sacrifice, and determined to persevere at all costs. We are to love Him with all of our strength. And He wants us to be *emotionally* passionate — full of irrepressible joy, deep affection, and enthusiastic wonder. We are to love Him with all of our hearts.

For me, this call to feel deeply has required a paradigm shift. It has inspired significant changes in the way I respond to God, both privately and publicly. As a disciple and pastor, I've become convinced that even though emotionalism is a danger, the greater danger for me — and for most in my neighborhood — is a shut-down, closed-up heart.

If these wild calls to passion still strike you as misplaced or irreverent, consider that when it comes to spreading the gospel, passionate expression may be an asset rather than a liability.

My wife's father, a determined non-Christian, once told her flatly, "If I believed what you people believe, I'd be on my knees pleading with every single person to hear me out and buy my line!" To him, very much an outsider, our reserve was incongruent with our message.

Put more positively, many outsiders visiting Bridgeway Church have been captivated by the passion of our people as they worship with intimacy, affection, and joy. Passionate people go well together with mercy, forgiveness, and eternal life.

Intensity in the church makes sense — not only for the way it will attract others but also for the fruit it will produce in your life and in your soul.

The Fruit of Passion

When you allow yourself to freely feel and express emotion, something precious inside your heart is given freedom as well. The nature and truth of your relationship with God are revealed to others and to yourself. Yet emotion also flows in the opposite direction. Your passion enables God to pour His new wine into your wineskin.

Once you get past your fear of feelings and begin to make room for your emotions in your personal life, small groups, and congregational gatherings, you'll find that they help produce rich contributions to your life with God. The fruit of restored passion is significant.

When you experience the fusion of Word and Spirit and release the biblical emotion of life with God, you're likely to see a dramatic increase in one or more of the following enriching and strengthening components of spiritual life.

Romance

Many are discovering (or rediscovering) the love of God — His Shepherd love, Father love, Brother love, Friend love, Bridegroom love. Listen to what's being sung. Read what's being written. Hear what's being discussed, especially among young leaders and believers. You'll see a widespread rediscovery of God's love for us.

Is this significant? Yes! From all biblical accounts, God's love is the spring from which our ability to love Him and others flows: "Love comes from God. Everyone who loves has been born of God and knows God" (1 John 4:7).

When it comes to love, we are like mirrors. We can only reflect what we've received.

Joy

Visit any growing church. Listen to any recent worship playlist on Amazon. Watch any worship video on YouTube. Look in any place students gather for worship or fellowship. You will see that young people have been broadly touched by the rising tide of passion, and the result is irrepressible joy. From a biblical perspective, joy is a wonderful thing! It's the fruit of the Spirit. It's our strength. It's our privilege. And perhaps most important of all, it is our most effective testimony to the outside world.

Worship

At conferences, in churches, and in small groups, people are worshiping as never before. They are praising God with their whole being — mind, heart, and body. We are seeing the kind of expressive, enthusiastic worship that before could only be imagined through the words of Scripture.

As Dr. Robert E. Webber, professor of theology at Wheaton College, says, "We want God to break into the world and touch our lives and our churches so we can sense God's presence. We want God's power — a power like the Resurrection and Pentecost — to fill our church with new life and hope."[1]

Praise and thanksgiving are not only emerging as a prominent part of our personal and corporate lives, but they are also becoming a more common reality in our hearts. Once again we are beginning to feel the wonder, justice, kindness, and goodness of God.

Music

As we renew and expand our welcome of the Holy Spirit, we are seeing an explosion of new music — according to Scripture, a sign of spiritual vigor (see Psalms 33:3; 40:3; 96:1; 144:9; 149:1). Hundreds of new worship songs have been released in the past twenty years.

Listen to the lyrics of this new music. You'll hear the connection to a longing for more of God — more of His tangible touch, more of the promised ministry of the Spirit, and more intimacy with Him. Consider this example from Brad Kilman:

> Oh, I want more of You, Living Water rain down on me Oh, I need more of You, Living Breath of Life
>
> Come and fill me up. . . .
>
> We are hungry, we are hungry
>
> We are hungry for more of You.
>
> We are thirsty, Oh Jesus.
>
> We are thirsty for more of You.[2]

And these lyrics from Charlie Hall, a worship leader for the Passion worship gatherings:

> Salvation spring up from the ground
>
> Lord rend the heavens and come down
>
> Seek the lost and heal the lame
>
> Jesus bring glory to your name.[3]

As in past renewals and revivals, new music is everywhere, and it's full of wonder, affection, and devotion.

Holy living

I've heard that Lorne Sanny, former international president of the Navigators, used to remind his staff, "Don't underestimate emotion. Emotion is that which ignites motion."

This fresh awakening of feeling is generating more than words and music. It's igniting deep devotion. It's releasing fierce desire for righteousness — integrity, purity, mercy, compassion, and justice. It's kindling a passion for mission and service. There is fresh energy, determination, and perseverance.

This renewed passion produced the bold courage of several of the victims at the Columbine High School tragedy in 1999. It launched the "pure till marriage" movement among millions of students. It is releasing a fresh flow of evangelism, hunger for the Scriptures, enthusiasm for prayer and fasting, and willingness for missionary service. It is inspiring generosity, hospitality, and simple living. It is propagating an all-your-heart love that is transforming millions of lives in wonderful ways.

Holy Affections

In the early days of the church in America, our nation experienced another Word-Spirit movement with a similar release of God's presence and passion. The response was the same then as it is now: Some embraced it enthusiastically; others were skeptical.

In the midst of the controversy, Jonathan Edwards, then a prominent evangelical pastor and now considered by many as having the finest theological mind in American history, wrote:

> I am bold to assert that no change of religious nature will ever take place unless the affections are moved. Without this, no natural man will earnestly seek for his salvation. Without this,

there is no wrestling with God in prayer for mercy. No one is humbled and brought to the feet of God unless he has seen for himself his own unworthiness. No one will ever be induced to fly in refuge to Christ as long as his heart remains unaffected. Likewise, no saint has been weaned out of the cold and lifeless state of mind, or recovered from backsliding, without having his heart affected. In summary, nothing significant ever changed the life of anyone when the heart was not deeply affected.[4]

When Jonathan Edwards writes of religious affections, he makes it very clear that he is thinking of something far deeper than fleeting feelings and emotions. He is speaking of the most determined convictions and decisions of the heart. And when convictions and decisions are deep enough to become our driving affections, we feel them. There is emotion. There is intensity. There is expression. This is the passion God is restoring by giving us firsthand experience with Him through the power of the Holy Spirit. It is not what we've in the past thought it to be — an emotional, unstable reaction to what is happening around us or something "those Spirit people" do in an emotional attempt to connect with God. Passion is one of the pieces of our spiritual puzzles, a key God hands us to unlock the deeper blessings of life with Him. It ignites our devotion and gives us an all-your-heart, all-your-mind, all-your-strength love for Him. It is His way to give us back our heart for Him.

God's purpose for passion is to help make us whole — to complete the picture of our spiritual lives and all the wonderful plans He has for us.

And hand in hand with passion goes another vital piece of our puzzle: experience.

CHAPTER 11

THE VALUE OF EXPERIENCE

In his best seller *Bringing Up Boys*, Dr. James Dobson explains how vital it is that a father be physically present with his children — available to talk, hold, and help his kids. Then he tells this story about his own father:

> I was blessed to have a wonderful father who was accessible to me from the earliest years of childhood. I'm told that when I was two years of age, my family lived in a one-bedroom apartment, and my little bed was located beside that of my parents. My father said later that it was very common during that time for him to awaken at night to a little voice that was whispering, "Daddy? Daddy?" My father would answer quietly, "What, Jimmy?" And I would say, "Hold my hand!" Dad would reach across the darkness and grope for my little hand, finally just engulfing it in his own. He said the instant he had my hand firmly in his grip, my arm would become limp and my breathing deep and regular. I'd immediately gone back to sleep. You see, I only wanted to know that he was there![1]

What's true for us physically is also true spiritually. We just want to know that our Father is there. We need to be touched to know that things are really okay. And when we are tangibly touched, it's much easier for our breathing to become "deep and regular."

David sang about the touch of God's goodness and how it makes breathing easy:

> *You have filled my heart with greater joy than when their grain*
> *and new wine abound.*

I will lie down and sleep in peace, for you alone, O LORD, make
me dwell in safety.

(Psalm 4:7-8)

From the time we are newborns — physically and spiritually — we need touch to survive. This is why experiencing God is so vital. It's why God has preserved so many fingers with which to touch us today. And it's why it is so important that we recover our willingness and ability to let those fingers touch us regularly.

We've Lost Touch

I'd like you to conduct a little experiment. Pull aside a friend (preferably an understanding one) who is firmly rooted in the evangelical tradition. Ask him if you can ask him a few questions, about his life with God. Then ask some questions like these.

- When was the last time you received a clear, specific answer to prayer?

- When was the last time you saw God do something undeniably supernatural?

- When was the last time God spoke personally to you?

- When was the last time you experienced God's presence in a tangible way?

I'll bet the response will be a blank stare followed by an expression of concern. The blank stare is because your friend likely hasn't seen anything happen and doesn't even know what you're talking about. And the concerned look is because your questions may leave him worried about your state of mind.

In large parts of the Word neighborhood, personal experience with God is very much a lost piece of spiritual life. When we get sick, our first response is to go to the doctor. When we need direction, our first call is to a friend or counselor. Most of us don't even consider going straight to God with our problems. Without intending to do so, we've become theologically orthodox in what we say but deists in what we do. Bill Bright, the late president of Campus Crusade for Christ, reportedly put it to his staff in even stronger terms: "Theologically, we are orthodox, but we are often practicing atheists!"

What has happened to personal experience with God in the Word church?

It has been jailed under suspicion of a broad range of mischief. The charges usually stem from one of these four categories:

- *Our discomfort with mystery.* The fact is that many of the ways God touches us are hard to explain, difficult to predict, and impossible to control. For those of us who want control and prefer stability, mystery is always uncomfortable and often unbearable. It is easier to limit ourselves to teaching and doing things we can promise and deliver without uncertainty.

- *Our desire to protect.* When we pray for the sick, not all are healed. When we try to impart spiritual gifts, not all receive. In hopes of sparing people the disappointment and disillusionment that can come when hopes go unfulfilled, we often avoid teaching about personal experience with God.

- *Our sense of outrage.* We have all seen or heard of excesses and abuses in the realm of experiencing God. False teaching, misinterpretation, and poor application have left people traumatized. The safe but sterile solution has been to shut the door.

- *Our natural worldview.* The respected, educated mind "knows" that reality is limited to what we can sense with our bodies and measure with our instruments. This is what we've been taught by parents, coaches, teachers, professional mentors, and government leaders — if not by words, then certainly by example. We view life through a natural, rather than supernatural, lens. We assume, consciously or not, that God is uninvolved.

Each of these concepts makes sense on the surface. Some are even rooted in good intentions. They are the reason so many who dwell in the Word neighborhood, myself included, have found it easy to lock up the idea of personal experience with God. Maybe it's been the same for you.

But is this what God wants from us? If you return to your Bible for another review of the evidence of God's power found in Scripture, you'll discover an emphatic, "No!"

The Biblical Call to Experience

Think of the role of personal experience in the life of every major hero of the faith in the Old Testament. In the first book of the Bible, we see God walking with Adam in the garden (see Genesis 2–3), speaking with Noah about the coming flood and the design of the ark (see Genesis 6–7), and visiting Isaac repeatedly (see Genesis 26). Jacob had his stairway to heaven and dislocated hip (see Genesis 28:10-22; 32:22-32). Joseph had his dreams and timely interpretations (see Genesis 37:2-11; 40–41).

Abraham had visions, dreams, audible voices, and physical encounters with his Father in heaven. God gave him a son through his sterile wife (see Genesis 21:1-3). A few years later, God spoke again. Abraham believed so strongly that he was hearing the direct word of God that he was willing to sacrifice his only son, Isaac, in order to remain obedient to the Lord. Only when an angel interceded did he put down the knife.

Clearly, Abraham was a man who understood the meaning of personal experience with God. And God blessed Abraham and his descendants greatly because of his faithfulness (see Genesis 22:1-18).

There are so many more: Moses' burning bush; Joshua's Jericho walls; Gideon's angelic visitations and fleeces; David's direct conversations; Solomon's visible encounters; and the prophets' visions.

The evidence is just as apparent in the New Testament. John the Baptist heard "the word of God" (Luke 3:2), saw "the Spirit come down from heaven as a dove" (John 1:32), and was told that "the man on whom you see the Spirit come down and remain is he who will baptize with the Holy Spirit" (John 1:33). Many others also had direct encounters with God: Elizabeth and Zechariah (see Luke 1:5-25), Simeon and Anna (see Luke 2:21-40), the Galatians, the Philippians, the Thessalonians, the Corinthians, and John with his magnificent vision on Patmos. And, of course, everyone who came into contact with the Lord of lords and King of kings, Jesus Christ— God in human flesh.

Just about every story that fills the pages of Scripture describes God breaking into the lives of His people in a dramatic, personal manner: visions, dreams, angels, prophetic messages, healings, exorcisms, unexplainable provision, mysterious protection, unexpected victory. The Bible is a book of stories about God showing Himself in tangible ways. It is a journal of experiences with God and the life-changing effects these encounters had on those He touched.

There is a message for us here: God *wants* us to experience Him!

Falling in Love

But why? Why does God place so much emphasis on personal encounters with His people — with you and me?

Maybe it's because He knows that only through personal experience will a relationship thrive. And, even though it sounds incredible, this is what God desires more than anything — an intimate, loving, one-on-one *relationship* with each of us. He tells us, "Here I am! I stand at the door and knock. If anyone hears my voice and opens the door, I will come in and eat with him, and he with me" (Revelation 3:20).

Imagine trying to maintain an intimate relationship with someone you never see, hear, or touch. The idea is ludicrous. The saying "Out of sight, out of mind" certainly applies to this situation.

I knew Beverly Gaylord for three years before our relationship caught fire. It was three years of watching from a distance. It was three years of hearing about her from my father, mother, brother, and sisters. Bev lived for a time in my parents' home in California. My family immediately fell in love with her and began conspiring ways to connect the two of us and thereby graft her into the family.

But I lived in Georgia. All I had to go on were words — some spoken, others written. They were reports of Bev's love for God, devotion to people, servant heart, kindly way, and contagious enthusiasm. I did visit home occasionally for short vacations, but my encounters with Bev were brief and unmemorable.

My godly mother became so exasperated with me that in an unguarded moment, she declared, "But she looks great in a bikini!" It was the ultimate matchmaking tactic. Still, her efforts produced no response. No sparks flew.

Finally, during one Christmas season, I had a free day at home before I had to go back to Georgia. Bev happened to be visiting, so I invited her to spend the day in San Francisco. I'd never been there. Bev knew the town, so I asked her to show me around.

From dawn to dusk we were up close and personal. We did it all: cable cars, the zoo, the botanical gardens, city parks, Ghirardelli Square. We had dinner at Fisherman's Wharf. We watched the sun set behind the Golden Gate Bridge. Our conversation throughout the day was unexpectedly easy and fun.

Our last stop was the steep, twisting drive up to Telegraph Hill. There in the December mist we viewed the spectacular display of lights that twinkled from the city and surrounding bay. We stood there for a long time enjoying the breathtaking panorama.

I took Bev's hand. It was delightfully soft. She looked up and said, "A penny for your thoughts?"

As I turned to answer, she rose on her tiptoes and kissed me. It was the gentlest, sweetest thing imaginable.

My mind raced. I knew she loved God. She was devoted to ministry. My brothers and sisters said she was great fun. Mom said she looked great in a bikini. And she was a great kisser. What more could a man want?

I asked her to marry me on the spot.

Sure, three years of reports from home and a series of distant impressions had moved me to that point. But it was that single day of close, personal experience that pushed me over the edge. My response to Bev took a quantum leap after just a few hours of personal connection — and one unforgettable kiss!

I had known all *about* Bev, but it wasn't until I experienced her personally that I began to *know* her. For relationships marked by passionate affection, sustained desire, enduring devotion, and unbreakable trust, experience is essential. The human heart does not devote without experience. We fall in love with a *person*, not a set of propositions.

Yes, my proposal was impetuous. Impulsive. Impassioned. Life-changing.

But experience will do that to you.

By the way, Bev said yes — and we're still at it, four children and over forty-years later!

Benefits and Blessings

Personal experience with God does even more than build an intimate relationship. The blessings that flow out of our encounters with Him enhance every aspect of our lives.

If you are a Word person who is stepping into the Spirit neighborhood for the first time, don't run from opportunities to let God touch you — pursue them! Open your heart to at least the possibility that even today God delivers us from demonic torment, responds to healing prayer, is pleased by fully engaged worship, bestows miraculous spiritual gifts, and speaks directly to us. Consider the possibility that He may want to use *you* in some of these ways — and that your relationship with Him will grow because of it.

The following are just some of the significant benefits of personal experience with God.

Experience Builds Faith

Faith may begin with words, but it soars with experience:

Because he turned his ear to me, I will call on him as long as I live.

(Psalm 116:2)

When I was a young Christian, even after two years of excellent teaching, regular Bible reading, routine quiet times, dozens of memory verses, and the best apologetics available, I continued to struggle with doubts about God. Fortunately, the friend who led me to Christ understood the importance of seeing God work. He encouraged me to pray specific and immediate requests so that we would know if and when God answered.

One day he asked, "What would be a really tough one? What could we ask God to do that would be really hard — hard enough so that if it happened, you would know it was God?"

I thought for a moment. "The conversion of my Dad."

"Let' pray," he said.

We began praying that Dad would devote his life to Christ. It was a long shot. Through my growing-up years, Dad taught me with conviction that men made God, not vice versa. "There is no one out there," he would say. When I devoted my life to Christ and wrote home that I'd found God, he was sure I'd been misled.

During a quiet time one day, I had a sense that somehow Psalm 50:15 was for him:

Call upon me in the day of trouble;

I will deliver you, and you will honor me.

I sensed this was what I should ask God to do in my dad's life. I knew it would take some kind of severe trouble for him to seriously consider God.

Time passed with no sign of turning. More time passed without change.

Then, two years later, I received an unexpected letter:

Dear Bau [my father's special name for me]:

I have crossed the river. I have accepted Jesus Christ....

As you know, I have been doing my best to be a *great* wing commander — not just another wing commander but the greatest that ever tried the job. . . . (But) I made a mistake (A commander's "Rules" violation). . . .

The next week the OSI (Office of Special Investigation) came in and investigated. The report to General Gideon, my boss at 13th Air Force headquarters, was that I was guilty of a bad deed. So I was called on the carpet at 13th AF and almost got fired.I couldn't believe it! I was wrong. But I so loved this wing and was so bloodcurdlingly crushed by this OSI investigation — realizing this could shoot my whole career, embarrass the family, and crush my chances of higher assignments — I spent a day or two in goose pimples and cold sweat.

Then it dawned on me. This was a signal from God. Something told me to go away from the office and the people, although I had several people in the waiting room.

No sooner had I reached my trailer than I fell on my bed and found myself praying and thanking God for this tragic signal. Peace came over me in a wave. I no longer had the burn in my stomach. . . .I knelt and in my little hooch called out my acceptance of Jesus Christ as my Lord, Savior, guard, guide, and teacher. I wasn't in a cathedral. There was no altar. No man in robes broke bread or offered wine. But it was all there. I crossed the river in confidence and my heart went warm. I prayed and read for a long time — then slept deeply.

The next day I flew to my trial. General Gideon chewed me out and said he ought to fire me, but he had talked to General Brown and decided to charge the whole thing up to experience. So my prayers and trust were answered, and I am in a new phase of life.

Reading those words made every nerve in my body tingle. Here it was: Psalm 50:15 — the trouble, the divine rescue, and a changed heart. It actually happened! And I personally experienced God listening and responding by doing the "impossible."[2]

You can imagine my excitement. After all these years, Dad had connected with God — and I fully understood that the God I was following and calling others to follow really is there!

Experience Puts Us in Touch with Reality

Experience causes us to realize — not just give mental assent but know and accept deep in our souls — that life is supernatural. We genuinely understand that "our struggle is not against flesh and blood, but against the rulers, against the authorities, against the powers of this dark world and against the spiritual forces of evil in the heavenly realms" (Ephesians 6:12).

Through experience with God, we encounter the invisible world. As we hear it, see it, touch it, and smell it, we begin to see past the limited worldview of our culture. We begin to see that what is described in the Bible is still happening around us today.

Experience Ignites Full Devotion

Remember the story of Isaiah's vivid encounter with God (see Isaiah 6:1-8)? He "saw the Lord" (verse 1). He heard seraphs "calling to one another" (verse 3). He felt "doorposts and thresholds" shake and saw the temple fill with smoke (verse 4). He felt a live coal touch his lips.

Undoubtedly, Isaiah had heard much about God and had read countless scrolls about Him. But now he was personally experiencing Him. The result? Deep awakening - "I am a man of unclean lips" (verse 5) . And total devotion — "Here am I. Send me!" (verse 8).

This scene plays itself out again and again throughout the pages of Scripture. It is the story of Abraham, Jacob, Moses, Joshua, Isaiah, Jonah, Mary, the disciples, the apostle Paul, and many others. Biblical devotion seldom springs from words alone. It is usually the fruit of supernatural experience.

This is terribly significant for those of us from the Word neighborhood. Embracing a robust ministry of the Spirit means freedom to move beyond words and evidences — as valuable as both are — to *personal experiences* that evoke unshakable confidence and passionate pursuit.

Experience Brings Deep Comfort

When we are going through painful times, it is one thing to receive comforting words from another person. Relief jumps to an entirely different level when we hear directly from God.

When we moved from Colorado to Oklahoma City, our daughter Bethany left her closest friends and found herself in a very lonely place. She would go to her college campus, sit in class, eat lunch by herself in her car, come home to study, and go to bed. This process repeated day after day. She was in pain, and my assurances that "time will take care of it" weren't helping.

One evening, she paused to simply be quiet and listen to what God might say. During this time, the Lord gave her a vision. She saw herself in scraggly woods with gnarly trees. Everything around her was gray and barren. She was walking through those woods, afraid and lonely. Then her viewpoint changed. She saw herself and the scraggly woods from above. The woods were a burned-out circle surrounded by green forest. Though she was in a burn zone, she was headed for lushness and beauty.

A few days later, she sat down with me. "Dad, the Lord spoke to me. He showed me that I'm in a dry spot, but He's going to fix it. There's green ahead. There's friendship ahead. It's going to be all right." She was assuring me!

I'm sure you've suffered through terrible pain at some point in your life, either from a divorce, death of a child or close friend, loss of a job, illness, or any of a thousand other traumas. Life hurts. But the deepest hurt of all is the fear that rescue may never come. A personal encounter with God reassures us that He is near and ready to help.

Experience Provides Access to God's Power

For those of us who desperately desire to help people, the power of God is a wonderful thing. It means we have more to offer than wise words, personal service, and sincere comfort.

During my early years as a pastor, I knew that many in my congregation were completely crippled in a major life area. They were locked in bitter anger, shame, addictions, and more. Yet nothing in the medicine cabinet of our thoroughly orthodox evangelical ministry could cure their diseases. God had to come and touch them in ways found exclusively in the Spirit neighborhood. Fortunately, God is restoring this power of the Spirit to openhearted evangelicals who have the biblical maturity and character to use it well.

This is what happened to Becky. Tormented by irrational fears and fits of overwhelming rage, she struggled for years without relief. She even began planning suicide. Finally, she and her husband met with a renewed evangelical pastor.

The pastor asked many questions. He then told Becky that he discerned demonic torment.

Over the next few hours, the pastor addressed and ordered out thirteen spirits. Then he prayed, "Holy Spirit, come and fill Becky up."

Becky says she was immediately overcome: "For the next two hours, I couldn't move; but inside I was having visions… (the Lord) talked about His love for me and His good plan for my future and why all this had happened. Then there was deep peace."

The change inside Becky was profound and lasting. Today, she and her husband are leaders in an empowered evangelical church where she leads prophetic ministry and they teach in a training center together.

Experience Releases Boldness in Believers

We see the experience-boldness connection repeatedly in the early church. The rushing wind, fiery tongues, and miraculous prophesying at Pentecost produces Peter's courageous proclamation, "Therefore let all Israel be assured of this: God has made this Jesus, whom you crucified, both Lord and Christ" (Acts 2:36).

Do you ever wonder why we who know so much about God and eternity share so little about them with others? The reason for most of us is simple: We are embarrassed. When we think of an invisible God, heaven and hell, resurrection from the dead, and eternal life, we find ourselves thinking, *This sounds so stupid!* Deep inside, we suspect our message won't wash with others. At times, we wonder if we believe it ourselves.

Personal experience with God helps change all this.

When we are part of undeniable healing, obvious deliverance, a revealing prophecy, or a supernatural dream, we "get it." At the deepest level, we understand that Jesus really is the Way, the Truth, and the Life and that no one comes to the Father except through Him. And we discover a wonderful urgency to say so, especially to those who don't yet know it.

Experience Converts Unbelievers

If you trace the explosion of the gospel through the early church, you repeatedly see two elements working together: the truth of the Word and the power of the Spirit. Notice the connection in the ministry of Christ.

Jesus was going throughout all Galilee, *teaching* in their synagogues, and *proclaiming* the gospel of the kingdom, and *healing* every kind of disease and every kind of sickness among the people." (Mt 4:23, NASB, italics mine),

> We see the same connection in the early church. At Pentecost, there is the sound of rushing wind, the appearance of tongues of fire, and miraculous praise in unlearned languages. Peter preaches, and "those who accepted his message were baptized, and about three thousand were added to their number that day" (Acts 2:41).

When Peter heals the man born crippled and declares that the power comes from Christ, "many who heard the message believed, and the number of men grew to about five thousand" (Acts 4:4).

Later, Philip goes to Samaria and proclaims Christ: "When the crowds heard Philip and saw the miraculous signs he did, they all paid close attention to what he said" (Acts 8:6).

In the early church there is an imperfect but clearly discernible pattern: Where we see the truth of the Word confirmed by the power of the Spirit, unbelievers often see and believe (see Acts 2:1-41,43-47; 3:1–4:4; 5:12-14; 13:6-12; 14:1-4; 16:25-34; 19:1-7,11-20; 28:1-10).

God teaches through His Word, but He transforms hearts and minds by combining that teaching with vivid, personal encounters with Him. When truth is fused with power, the result is a convicting fire that won't be extinguished.

Experience Packs a Wallop

My son Bow has always been our family's straight arrow. He's always had an instinct for what is just and right. As a Little Leaguer, he'd move to the far end of the bench to avoid off-color humor. If our house rules favored one brother or sister over another, he'd press — quietly but tenaciously — for parity.

When it came time to deal with God, Bow responded promptly with trust and obedience. He believed and was baptized because it was the right thing to do. He paid attention in church. He was consistent with his daily quiet times. Bow does the right thing simply because it's right. If only life was that straightforward for the rest of us!

One day when he was sixteen, Bow joined Bev and me at a Spirit-people conference. During a message on intimacy with God, Bow recognized that something was missing from his right and dutiful life. And he wanted that missing piece.

When the ministry teams formed at the front, Bow stepped forward and asked for prayer. From his journal, here's his description of what happened:

> Today was probably the most exciting and growing-in-Christ day of my life. Today I got to experience God firsthand like never before. And I also got to pray for others, and while I was praying it just seemed like God came. I even went numb and shook some. It was really encouraging to hear Jan Bingaman prophesy over me about me praying and God healing others through me. And even after me and Jan prayed, Tiffany had her migraine headache go away. Tonight I realized that all I've learned about Jesus and God is true. And I want to experience Him more and more. For this is just the beginning of how God is going to use me in the days to come. Thank you, Jesus! Wow.[3]

What happened here? Simply put, a kid from the Word neighborhood ventured into the Spirit neighborhood and personally encountered God. He'd heard the stories, listened to the sermons, and absorbed the greatest preaching in the world for fifteen years (mine!). But this time, God touched him in a physical way. Then, on the heels of his encounter with the Spirit, Bow prayed for a young lady named Tiffany. To his amazement, her condition changed as he prayed.

First Bow felt the hand of God. Then he saw God do something undeniably supernatural. And he understood at a deeper level than ever before that everything he'd heard about God is true.

Experience packs a wallop.

Like Bow, you'll discover that a personal experience with God will change you. You'll want *in* — all the way in. You'll be hungry to experience Him more and more. You'll uncover passion you never knew you had.

This is the marvelous impact of the fusion of Word *and* Spirit. Isn't it just what you're looking for?

CHAPTER 12

THE SECRET'S OUT

One thing you will discover, if you haven't already, is that when you begin to learn new things about the power of the Spirit, others will find out. There's no way to keep it a secret.

People will see it in you. They will see it in your worship. Even if you don't raise your hands, they will see you engage at a different level. You will radiate fresh affection, confidence, and intimacy through your posture, your movement, your face, and your eyes.

People will notice it in the new books you forget to hide and the new places you're seen visiting. They'll hear it in your comments that slip out in unguarded conversation — fleeting references to laying hands on a sick child, sensing an oppressive spirit, sharing a message from God for a friend, feeling the Spirit's presence in worship.

No matter how hard you try to bottle it up, you'll leak renewal all around you. And those who aren't nearby will hear it from others. Let's face it: People talk. And when Word is fused with Spirit, people talk a lot. It's radical. It's different. It's fascinating. To many, it's frightening and even shocking. If you are changing your mind about the Spirit, it won't take long for your entire network of religious communities to find out and begin talking — a few to you, but most to others.

The good news is that after thirty-five years of Spirit revival and well over fifty million people who have crossed over the wall, we know a lot about what to expect when word of renewal gets out.[1]

The bad news is that the one common denominator in Spirit renewal is . . . drum roll . . . *opposition.*

Opposition can range from mild concern (the hope that you'll see your error and get over it quickly) to muffled criticism (you hear that "people are talking") to growing suspicion (you're no longer included or trusted in ministry decisions) to hostile expulsion (you are asked to leave the church, or the hope is that you'll go without being asked). This resistance may even come from those closest to you.

Surprised? If you've taken even the first few steps into the Spirit neighborhood, then you're probably not. Change is hard. Religious change is excruciating. Religious change that reveals the Spirit's power has been diabolically rigged to explode.

As you explore a new spiritual neighborhood and the exciting possibilities of the fusion of Word and Spirit, you too will likely encounter opposition. It may come from your family, your friends, fellow believers, or your pastor. It may come from all of them. I spent thirty years crossing the Word-Spirit wall in four different churches with results that ranged from dismal failure to moderate success. My experience tells me that you will likely face four pressing questions.

Question 1: What do I say?

When you begin to see and experience new dimensions of the Spirit's presence and power, you'll want to talk about it. How could you not? When you pray for people and see them healed, when you receive a genuine supernatural message that stuns both you and the person you're helping, when you see a demon leave a tormented person, you are going to want to tell somebody.

Who should you tell, and what should you say? And what about others who want to know what's going on?

My advice is simple: Say as little as possible.

Sure, you may have a few "safe" friends you know well and trust deeply. They will be good companions for your new spiritual journey. You also may have a Spirit friend or two who have seen what you're seeing and can encourage you along the way. But for most people, your disjointed stories, uncertain explanations, erroneous terminology, unrealistic expectations, and unbridled enthusiasm will leave them in shock. Most listeners will try to be polite but will leave frightened, confused, and angry.

After watching many go through the frustration of processing their early Spirit experiences with their evangelical friends, I'd recommend handling your new discoveries the way you'd treat an unfamiliar musical instrument: Practice lots in private before you play in public.

Give yourself time to search the Scriptures, put the biblical pieces together, form sensible conclusions, and find biblical words to describe what you're experiencing. Wait to see not only the *event* of your Spirit experiences but also the *pattern* of them. How often do they happen — or not happen? What are the causes? Are they always the same, or do they differ from time to time and setting to setting? Are the effects the same for all, or do different people report different results? What's lasting? What's the fruit in your life?

With that said, however, I realize that some people — a spouse, a close family member, a persistent friend — will need to know. When you must describe what's happening, how do you say it in a way that does the most good?

The principle for talking about your renewal is the same as for anything else: "[Speak] the truth in love" (Ephesians 4:15). There are several things to keep in mind as you do this:

- *Simply tell your story.* Describe what you are discovering in the Bible. Explain what you are seeing or experiencing. Be as specific and accurate as you can— no exaggerating. Relate what you are reading that's been helpful. Describe how your thinking is changing and what remains unmoved. Stick with "I" messages and avoid the temptation to tell others what they ought to be thinking and doing. Telling your Spirit story to others is a lot like teaching your kids about sex: Just give them what they need for the time being. Anything more than that is usually counterproductive.

- *Speak their language.* A common and often alienating mistake in sharing Spirit discoveries is to use the jargon of the Spirit church. Just think about your own past reaction to comments such as, "The manifest Presence of God filled the room, and we were all baptized in the Spirit. Then holy laughter broke out, and several were slain in the Spirit. I went into my prayer language, and a highly anointed sister gave me an awesome prophetic word." When speaking to people who are new to renewal or skeptical about the Spirit side of the church, avoid confusing jargon and use their language as much as possible.

- *Appreciate your heritage.* It's easy to imply that all you've been taught in the past is defective and useless. It's also easy to come across as superior to your fellow believers. I recommend that you very intentionally value your past. It's also good to distinguish yourself from the stereotypes you know are spinning in your listener's mind. I usually make it clear that I don't speak in tongues, that I know God heals only sometimes, that I know committed Christians are not always prosperous in business, and that I'm convinced not all nagging evil is from tormenting spirits. You'd be amazed how reassuring these kinds of statements are to those who believe all Spirit people think and act alike.

Question 2: How do I respond to the critics?

As discreet as you may be about your renewal, as hard as you may work at being clear and correct with your words, as humble as you may be about your exploring, and as nonpushy as you may be in your enthusiasm, you will have critics. They may be close friends, family members, ministry colleagues, former mentors, or church leaders. How will you respond to them?

Again, my answer is simple: As much as possible, avoid it.

As you share about your journey, you'll probably discover two groups who are keenly interested: seekers and arguers. The seekers may range from eager to skeptical, but they genuinely want to know what you are seeing, what's real, and — if it is real — how they can get in on it. Seekers listen carefully. They check you out. They ask about the details of what happened. They read the Bible passages, articles, and books you suggest. They go with you to the places you are visiting to learn more.

Seekers are new wineskins. Their hearts and minds are open, and they actively join you in exploring for truth — even new truth that may challenge long- standing thinking and practice. Responding to the questions and reservations of seekers is worthwhile for them because they'll learn from you, and it is worthwhile for you because they'll keep you honest and balanced.

Arguers, on the other hand, are determined to argue. Out of some confluence of prior study, respected teaching, personality bent, personal experience, loyalty to tradition, and/or past trauma, arguers are certain they know the truth about the Spirit and His ways. And they know you are wrong. They feel obligated to correct your thinking and personally responsible for protecting others from your influence.

I have seen arguers change their minds. But I have never seen an arguer change his mind through listening to renewal stories, reading renewal books, or discussing Scripture. Thus, I suggest my avoid-when-possible strategy for responding to arguers. Otherwise you are likely destined for frustration, growing animosity, and broken friendships.

At one church where I was previously pastor, there was an elder who was both a good friend and a determined opponent of Spirit renewal. One night he took me aside. Speaking in an intense, quiet voice, he said, "Listen, bro, I know you are thinking a lot about gifts of the Spirit and other charismatic stuff. To be honest, I don't want to think about it. I don't want to talk about it. I don't want us to change anything about the way we are doing things in this area. We have more important things to do around here. Now, I know I can't tell you to stop. But do me and the rest of us elders a favor. When you go places to learn about these Holy Spirit things, just keep it quiet. Don't tell the people. You'll spook the sheep. And don't tell us."

In a perfect world, my advice in regard to this wouldn't be necessary. But we don't live in a perfect world; and some conversations are, in fact, well worth avoiding. An argument with an arguer about the Holy Spirit is one of them.

For the most part, I took the elder's advice. I kept most of my friends and had a good working relationship with the elders for as long as I was at that church.

At times, however, it is impossible to avoid explaining yourself to determined opponents. If, for example, your renewal journey begins to affect a church or local ministry, you owe it to the leaders to explain what's happening, assure them of your willingness to abide by their guidelines, and do all you can to protect the health and welfare of the community (see Ephesians 4:1-3). You give yourself the best shot at a favorable response if you take the following actions:

- *Tell your story.* Explain what is happening. Tell them what you are rediscovering. Describe how it's impacting your life. Let them know you still have lots to learn.

- *Affirm your commitment to go by the Book.* Let them know what you are doing to keep your exploring centered in the Bible.

- *Value your common ground.* Help your critics see that you are not renouncing the strengths of your past. Make it clear that in your search for missing pieces, you're still holding on to the biblical "main things" — intimacy with God, holy character, loving community, and discipling others.

- *Respect the community leadership.* Assure the leaders that you are eager to hear any counsel that those with experience, maturity, or authority are willing to give. Offer to keep them informed. And assure them that you'll abide by their guidelines or withdraw in a way that best protects the continued strength of the community.

Believe me, I have lived through significant strains among leadership teams and church congregations over "Spirit issues." If you keep a gentle tone, a patient pace, and a respectful manner, you can often continue to grow in the Spirit personally, share your discoveries with others, and see your community come to embrace more of the Spirit's powerful provision.

Question 3: How do I introduce Spirit renewal to my church?

Discovering the power of the Spirit is much like discovering the love of the Father and the grace of Jesus. You want to share it with others. Because of our religious civil war, however, introducing the Spirit to some Word congregations is like persuading post-Appomattox Southerners to love Abraham Lincoln. It can be a tough sell.

So how should you begin? Here's my advice: Start small and safe.

I don't recommend beginning with a mass exorcism followed by public prophecy open to any and all in the main worship service. Likewise a good old-fashioned Pentecostal "get 'em baptized in the Spirit and teach 'em all to speak in tongues" program at the annual youth retreat isn't usually the best first step. Just as there are good and not-so-good ways to feed pigeons (slow and quiet versus yelling loudly and waving your arms), there are wise and not-so-wise ways to help Word people embrace the lost ministries of the Spirit.

The best place to begin is in your own personal ministry. Don't start by trying to sell words and theories about the Spirit's power. Just act on it — kindly, patiently, and persistently without lengthy defense or explanation. When you notice sick people, offer to pray for them. If appropriate (and it usually is), pray for them right there that God will heal them directly and completely. Not all will be healed, of course, but you — and they — will be amazed at how many times God does something memorable.

When you pray with people, pause to listen to the Spirit. Explain that you want to start by simply being quiet and asking the Spirit to reveal what the Father wants to do. People will understand and appreciate it.

More important, as you listen and pay attention to what appears on the screen of your mind, you'll notice that the Spirit speaks far more often than you ever imagined. Try it. The next time you pray for someone, take a full two minutes to simply listen. Assume He's really there and wants to help you "pray in the Spirit" (Ephesians 6:18). Jot down what comes to mind. Perhaps it's a verse of Scripture. Perhaps it's a word or a picture or a feeling. Now use it as you pray. You'll be amazed at how often the person will say, "How did you know?"

By far, the best way to make room for Spirit ministry in your church is simply to do it, let God work, and let the word spread through those you touch.

If you have the influence and energy to try something corporately, both common sense and successful church renewals suggest that the best place to start is with something familiar and agreeable. At two of my previous churches, we began with an alternative service that created a place for intimate worship. The affectionate worship ignited hunger for more — more of whatever was available, more of God. Soon all kinds of new, strange, and wonderful things were happening. It was a dream come true to some and an outrageous scandal to others. Intimate worship is a great place to begin experiencing God.

If I were doing it again, however, I'd start with something even easier to initiate than a new worship service. I would request an opportunity to train a listening prayer team and offer prayer after worship services. By listening prayer, I mean that the team members listen for the Spirit's leading as they listen to the people's requests. They may hear nothing beyond what the person requests. But sometimes the Spirit will reveal a word, a picture, or a verse that hints at a deeper need.

As your team follows the Spirit's leading, God will begin to work in remarkable ways. The congregation will experience hearing God's voice in a gentle, receivable way. Soon someone will be healed of a physical ailment. Another will experience emotional healing as deep wounds are exposed. Eventually, the team will discern and bind an oppressing spirit, and someone will experience dramatic freedom from long-standing torment.

Gradually, both the prayer team and the church will develop a history of experience with God and the power of His Spirit. Without any formal change of doctrine or dramatic pronouncement by the leaders, many will find themselves walking in the Spirit and seeing His promised power as they minister to others.

To light a fire of Spirit renewal in your church, I'd recommend you start with listening prayer — and watch what God does to reveal Himself.

Question 4: When should I find a new church?

Even after being respectful and humble, open and honest, and persistent and patient, it's possible that the leadership of your church simply will not want to explore the Spirit neighborhood. They won't want you doing Spirit ministry, either personally or corporately. They won't want you sharing your story with others.

At this point, you either have to rebel, stop your renewal process, or go to a different church. When those are your options, it's usually best to move on.

I've left churches twice myself, and I can testify that it was traumatic both times. Because church was my profession, it involved geographic transplants, which were excruciating not only for me but also for my wife and four children. For me, it meant starting over in salary and benefits. For all of us, it involved leaving best friends with tearful fare-wells.

For me, it also included strong feelings of confusion, injustice, grief, anger, and failure. Leaving a church is a painful thing. But sometimes it is God's best for everyone. Looking back, I wouldn't have missed the opportunities I had in any of the churches I served, and I wouldn't have stayed at any church I left. I am convinced God leads both to and away.

If this becomes your experience, it's vital to your spiritual, emotional, and physical health that you remember a few points about the church you are leaving:

- That church did you and your family significant good through the years you were there. Be sure to say a heartfelt thanks to both the people there and to God as you leave.

- God will continue to love and bless that church despite their skepticism about your renewal. God is the "Lord, the compassionate and gracious God, slow to anger, abounding in love and faithfulness, maintaining love to thousands, and forgiving wickedness, rebellion and sin" (Exodus 34:6- 7). Despite their reluctance to recover their missing Spirit pieces, God will simply work through whatever pieces they will receive. It's amazing how little we have to get right for God to love and bless us. And aren't we all glad for that!

- That church is still, in a very real sense, your "family" even after you leave. Wherever you go from there, you are to "be devoted to one another in brotherly love. Honor one another above yourselves" (Romans 12:10). Remember what drew you there in the first place and kept you there so long. Speak well of the leaders, people, and place.

If you do these things, you can always go back for a visit and enjoy good memories. Good friends and a clean conscience are worth preserving.

As for finding a new church, you'll probably want to look for these essentials:

- They preach the Word. In embracing the power of the Spirit, you don't want to lose your devotion to the truth of the Word. Find a church where the pastor is a strong Bible teacher who motivates you to continue to read it for yourself.

- They welcome the power of the Spirit. Look for active ministries that encourage healing prayer, hearing God's voice, seeking and developing spiritual gifts, and heartfelt worship.

- They keep their focus on what matters most. Although they appreciate the incredible value of both Word and Spirit, they realize these are just the means. Jesus is the end. They are devoted to Him and the primary goals of knowing God, developing holy character, loving one another, and making disciples of all nations.

- They equip the saints. Wherever you go, you want to be trained, valued, put on the field, and allowed to "play." Look to see if they have a strong network of home groups. These are ideal training grounds for Spirit ministry and personal care. Look for some kind of training center where people systematically teach and practice things such as hearing God's voice, healing prayer, spiritual warfare, time alone with God, sharing the gospel, following up with new believers, and other practical ministry skills. You want to be taught and encouraged to use the newly discovered power of the Spirit to do what God has created you to do.

With the growing number of Word-Spirit churches, chances are good there is one near you looking for people just like you. If not, perhaps you can help start one!

That's exactly what happened with Ted and Pat, good friends of mine who found themselves both loving their evangelical roots and longing for a more experiential life in the Spirit. In their search, Ted and Pat eventually found themselves at a Spirit conference. Ministry teams were inviting those with physical ailments to receive prayer for healing.

Ted and Pat both qualified. Ted suffered from esophageal reflux so intensely that for years he had slept only while sitting up. Pat had chronic back pain. Hesitantly, they went forward.

As the ministry team prayed for Ted, he opened his hands and heart to whatever the Lord wanted to do. Ted describes what happened next: "I was overcome. I couldn't stand. The next thing I knew, I was on the floor. I felt like I'd been plugged into a wall socket. Something like electricity was coursing through my body, and I began to shake uncontrollably."

This went on for about ten minutes. Then Ted lay on the floor, apparently unconscious, for another half hour. He could hear but couldn't move — or more accurately, he did not want to move. He was filled with an amazing sense of peace and of the presence of God.

In the days that followed, Ted's esophageal reflux slowly but steadily receded.

Within a few weeks, it was gone, never to return.

At the same time, Ted was on the floor, another ministry team was praying for Pat. She felt nothing dramatic — except that her back pain suddenly and completely disappeared. It never came back.

Not long after, Ted and Pat helped launch a new church that embraces both the truth of Scripture and the power of the Spirit. Today, they are living examples of the wonderful things that happen when we enter a new neighborhood and experience God through the union of Word and Spirit.

EPILOGUE.
MORE – AND
STILL MORE

I've already told you the story of Ed Powell, my Air Force Academy roommate, helping me memorize my first passage of Scripture: "And this is the testimony: God has given us eternal life, and this life is in his Son. He who has the Son has life; he who does not have the Son of God does not have life" (1 John 5:11-12).

With Ed's encouragement, I finally got that verse down word for word. I figured I was finished. I had my spiritual birth certificate. I was not only in the faith but also in the Navigators.

Not so! Little did I know that joining Ed and the Navigators meant my days of memorizing Scripture were just beginning. After that first verse came another and another and another. I soon embarked on learning the entire Topical Memory System — at that time 109 verses!

I thought they would never end. Yet with every verse I committed to memory, my spiritual maturity and insight into the ways of God grew. It was an amazing, exciting time for deepening the understanding of my faith.

Recovering your missing pieces is a little like my memorizing Scripture with the Navigators. It's a journey that continues for a lifetime.

We've talked about how some of your missing pieces are waiting for you on the other side of the Word-Spirit wall. If you've grown up in the evangelical tradition, you'll benefit from what you've missed on the Spirit side. If you were born and raised as a charismatic, you'll discover the benefits of a Word approach. Either way, God is inviting you to climb over the wall and learn from the other half of your spiritual family. He's holding out a piece that will fill a large hole in your puzzle.

And here's the wonderful thing about God: He never stops. The working power of the Spirit, or the life-giving truth of the Word, is not the only piece missing from your picture of God. For the rest of your life, He will faithfully come after you and offer pieces that will result in new and greater blessings — and will draw you closer to Him.

It might be a revelation that helps you make more sense of life. It might be a way to know joy even in the midst of trials. It might be a life-changing discovery that you are meant to share with others. It might be the joy of leading someone to Christ. It might be the reality that "two are better than one" (Ecclesiastes 4:9). It might be the honor of protecting the oppressed. Whatever it is, you can rely on an infinite God to offer opportunities to continue growing. One of the great privileges of membership in His kingdom is the fact that there will always be more.

Paul said as much to the early believers at Philippi: "And this is my prayer: that your love may abound *more and more* in knowledge and depth of insight, so that you may be able to discern what is best and may be pure and blameless until the day of Christ" (Philippians 1:9-10, emphasis added).

As long as we are discerning enough to recognize that there is more to God than we know and humble enough to learn from others, especially those from other neighborhoods, we can look forward to unending, invigorating renewal. And with each new piece will come a fresh surge of hunger, confidence, and delighted wonder.

A bonfire awaits you. God is already stirring hearts around the world, fusing Word and Spirit for His glory, and leading His children into a powerful, joyful, and complete relationship with Him.

This is exactly what I was looking for all those years. I believe it's what you're seeking too — and exactly what God intends for your future.

Won't you join me?

STUDY GUIDE

Now the Bereans were of more noble character than the Thessalonians, for they received the message with great eagerness and examined the Scriptures every day to see if what Paul said was true.

Acts 17:11

Learning new things from God requires two equally important commitments: a humble heart to receive "with great eagerness" and a diligent mind to "examine the Scriptures." When it comes to recovering our understanding of the promised power of the Spirit, we need both a teachable heart and a searching mind. This study guide is designed to help you cultivate both head and heart, either alone or with a small group of fellow explorers.

For each of the twelve chapters, there is an opportunity for "Searching the Scriptures" in the often-unexplored area of the Holy Spirit. As you work through this study, you will look at many of the important passages in both the Old and New Testaments that teach us about the Spirit — who He is and how He helps. Whether you are in a small group or reading this book on your own, this study will help to fill in the gaps in your understanding of what God wants to do in your life by giving you His Spirit.

Also for each of the chapters, as well as the introduction and epilogue, there are questions for "Sharing Your Life." These are designed to help a small group read the book and process the ideas together. If you are reading the book alone, these questions will help you think more personally and practically about what to do with the ideas you may be encountering for the first time.

Whether you are reading the book by yourself or with a group, work through the study and the application questions. If you will engage both your mind and heart, you'll discover there is a lot more to the promised power of the Spirit than you ever imagined!

INTRODUCTION

More! Encouraging those who love the Bible to experience the promised power of the Spirit

1. Why did you pick up this book? What interests you about *The Promised Power: Experiencing the Union of Word* and *Spirit*?

2. How are you feeling about exploring this subject and discussing it with others?

3. This book is about pursuing all that God provides through two great means: His Word and His Spirit. Describe your personal experience with each. Which is easier for you to talk about? What makes the other more difficult?

4. "Something's missing — there's got to be more." Have you ever thought this way about your life with God? If so, what did you mean? What did you sense was missing?

5. Have you ever experienced God— seen Him work, heard His voice, felt His touch? If so, what happened, and how did it affect you?

CHAPTER 1: A Whole New Floor

Searching the Scriptures.

The Holy Spirit – Who Is He?

Most of us can begin to understand God the Father because we have a father on earth who to a greater or lesser extent reflects his love and care. Most of us can likewise begin to understand God the Son because we have His story and know He looks something like us. But when it comes to God the Spirit, most of us draw a blank. Although the Bible gives us a few metaphors (for example, wind, fire, water, oil, and a dove), there is no person or thing that gives us a clear picture of what He is like or how He works. Nevertheless, let's begin by taking a look at what the Bible tells us about this wonderful and very "other worldly" Person.

- *What He's like.* Read the following passages and summarize what each tells us about the attributes of the Holy Spirit: Genesis 1:2; Psalm 139:7-12; Isaiah 11:1-3; 1 Corinthians 2:6-16.

- *What He has done.* What do the following passages tell us about what the Holy Spirit has done in the past? Job 33:4; Psalm 104:30; Luke 1:35; Romans 8:11; 2 Peter 1:20-21

- *Who He is.* What do the following verses tell us about the Spirit's identity? Matthew 28:18-20; Act 5:3-4; 16:7; 1 Corinthians 6:9-11; 2 Corinthians 13:14

Sharing Your Life.

1. If you imagine the church as a town divided by railroad tracks into a Word neighborhood and a Spirit neighborhood, which side of the tracks did you come from?

2. What do you know and how do you feel about the other side? What (or who) has most deeply shaped your attitudes toward the other side?

3. Have you ever visited the other side by reading a book, making a close friend, or attending an event? If so, what

was the experience like for you? If not, what has kept you away?

4. How would you describe where you are in the process of putting together the truth of the Word and the power of the Spirit in your own life with God? In your ministry to others?

CHAPTER 2: Filling the Void

Searching the Scriptures.

The Holy Spirit – His Power in the Old Testament

When John the Baptist announced to the Jewish nation that Someone was coming who would "baptize [them] with the Holy Spirit and with fire" (Matthew 3:11; Luke 3:16), the people were electric with anticipation. Based on what they knew about the Holy Spirit from the stories and prophecies of their Scriptures, they saw the coming of the Spirit to all believers as a staggering wonder. They easily imagined the dramatic difference the Spirit would make in every life He invaded.

For most of us, the idea of the coming of the Spirit evokes little more than a yawn because we have so little background in the powerful impact He makes. To catch up to the people of Jesus' day in our understanding of the power of the Spirit, it's good to read what they had read.

- Read the following passages and describe what each teaches about the impact of the Spirit on those He empowers: Exodus 31:1-11; Numbers 11:16-17,24-30; Judges 3:10; 15:9-17; 1 Samuel 10:1-11; 11:6-8; 16:11-13; 2 Chronicles 15:1-8; 20:14-17; Nehemiah 9:19-20,29-30; Ezekiel 2:1-8; Micah 3:8-12.

- Summarize what we learn about the power of the Spirit from the Old Testament stories. When the Spirit came on a person, what kinds of things happened?

Sharing Your Life

1. Briefly tell your spiritual story — how you first started thinking personally about God and what has happened since then to bring you to where you are today.

2. As you think back on your history with God, who and what have been the primary influences? What have you come to believe most deeply? What are you presently doing to pursue and please God?

3. As you think about those who have helped you spiritually, what were their greatest strengths, and how did these strengths impact you?

4. As you reflect on your spiritual heritage, did you ever have a sense that something was missing? If so, what was missing? How and when did you sense the gaps?

CHAPTER 3: Big Questions

Searching the Scriptures

Promises in the Old Testament

By the time of Jesus, the news that God would send His Spirit on all His people was not new. God had been repeating the promise and describing the impact for more than seven hundred years.

- As you look at the following promises from the prophets, see if you can identify the who, what, and when of each prophecy:

Who would receive the benefit, *what* would the impact of the Spirit's coming be, and *when* would the prophecy be fulfilled? Isaiah 44:1-3; Ezekiel 36:24-27 (compare with the new covenant promise in Jeremiah 31:31-34 and Hebrews 8:7- 13); Joel 2:28-32 (compare with Acts 2:14-39)

• Although all these prophesies will see their complete fulfillment in an outpouring of the Spirit when the Messiah returns at the end of this age, they tell us much about the kind of impact the Spirit has on all He touches. What do these prophecies teach us about what to expect from the Holy Spirit today?

Sharing Your Life

1. Cessationism is the theory that much of the miraculous power apparent in the early church ceased with the completion of the New Testament and the death of the original apostles (things such as healing the sick, discerning and expelling demons, hearing God directly, receiving prophetic visions and dreams, speaking and interpreting spiritual languages, and performing miracles). Have you heard of this theory? Have you seen it in practice? If so, what have you thought, and how have you felt?

2. In your Bible reading, have you noticed any significant differences between the way the people in the early church experienced God and the way you have experienced Him? If so, give some specific examples. Why do you think these differences exist?

3. Have you ever tried doing some of the clearly supernatural things you see in the New Testament? If so, what happened? If not, what has kept you from trying?

4. Have you ever experienced being painfully stuck in some area of your life? What spiritual tools have you used to deal with it? What were your results? Have you ever wondered if there might be some other approach that might help? If so, what other approach have you considered?

5. For one week, try the "green pen experiment" (see pages 121–122). As you read your Bible, mark in green anything that seems mysterious or supernatural (for example, healing, dreams, angels, expelling demons, prophesying, and so on). Notice what God does among the people in His Book and how often it is mentioned.

CHAPTER 4: Patterns of Missing Pieces

Searching the Scriptures

The Holy Spirit in Jesus' Life and Ministry

Although there are many things about Jesus' life that are unique to His identity as God the Son and to His mission as "the Anointed One" (Daniel 9:25), there is much about the Spirit's ministry to Him that foreshadows the Spirit's ministry to us. As you look at what the Spirit did for Jesus and for those around Him, remember that many of these stories are written "as examples . . . for us" (1 Corinthians 10:11). Think about what God is telling us through these stories about what we can expect the Spirit to do for us today. Then as you read Jesus' teaching about how the Spirit will help us, ask yourself, *How much of the promised power am I using in my life?*

- As you read the following passages from Luke, notice what the Spirit did for the people around Jesus: 1:11-17 (John the Baptist); 1:26-37 (Mary); 1:39-45 (Elizabeth); 1:67-79 (Zechariah); 2:25-32 (Simeon).

- According to the following passages, how did the Holy Spirit help Jesus? Matthew 12:22-32; Luke 3:21-23; 4:1-13; 4:14-21; Acts 10:37-38

- What does Jesus teach us about what we can expect the Spirit to do in our lives? See Luke 11:9-13; 24:45-49; John 7:37-39; 14:8-26; 15:26-27; 16:5-15; 20:19-23; Acts 1:1-8.

- From the pictures in these stories and the instructions from Jesus, what do you sense God is telling us about what we can expect the Spirit to do for us and for the people (believers and unbelievers) around us?

Sharing Your Life

1. If you did the "green pen experiment," what did you discover?

2. As you think about the story of Josiah, what do you see as important lessons for today?

3. Do you see any personal counterpart to the lost Book of the Law — any piece of spiritual life that is prominent in the Bible but largely missing in your life and among those in your spiritual family? If so, what is it?

4. Of the influences that commonly cause biblical truth and practice to disappear (culture, unwillingness, devaluation, obsolescence, overreaction, and so forth), which have you seen at work in your spiritual family? In your personal life?

5. Renewal is what happens when God gives back a missing piece of life with Him and we experience the resulting surge of life, joy, and hope. Where have you personally experienced renewal? How did it come? What was the impact on you?

CHAPTER 5: Awakening

Search the Scriptures

The Holy Spirit – In the Early Church

As we move to the stories of the early Christians, we see the Holy Spirit working among people just like us. Jesus had ascended to heaven and, as promised, poured out the Spirit on all who believed in Him (see Acts 2). The believers had been baptized with the Spirit as He came on them for the first time in response to their faith. The church was beginning its mission of being Jesus' witnesses first where they were and eventually "to the ends of the earth" (Acts 1:8). The leaders and people were starting to proclaim to a hostile and skeptical world the good news of forgiveness, the indwelling power of the Spirit, and the promise of future resurrection. With their words, they explained the message. Through the promised power of the Spirit, they confirmed the message through their transformed lives and stunning miracles. These are the stories about our immediate spiritual ancestors. They were part of the same body (the church) as we are. They bore the same label ("Christians") as we do. They were in the same age (the time between Christ's ascension and return) as we are. They were just like us. We are just like them. Let's look at how the Spirit worked among them to see what we might expect Him to do among us.

- Read Acts 2. This is the story of the first believers being "baptized with the Holy Spirit," according to Jesus' promise (Acts 1:5). Parts of this story are clearly intended to be unique. They mark this first outpouring of the Spirit as a monumental moment in history. (Notice the similarities between Acts 2 and the defining moments of past and future outpourings of the Spirit in Numbers 11:24-30 and Joel 2:28-32.) But parts of the Pentecost story mark a beginning of things that will continue. As you read the story, what do you sense God is telling us that applies to us today?

- The following passages give us God's descriptions of the Spirit's work among the early believers: Acts 4:8-11,31-35; 5:1-11; 6:1-7; 7:54-60; 8:14- 39; 9:17-25,31; 10:9-23,44-47; 11:15-18,27-30; 13:1-12,49-52; 15:22-29; 16:6-10; 19:1-7; 20:22-31; 21:7-14. As you read these stories, ask yourself three questions:

  1. What specifically did the Spirit do to help these people?

  2. What was the effect of His help on the people in the early church and on those outside the church?

  3. How much of this are you personally seeing today?

Sharing Your Life

  1. What differences have you noticed between the Spiritual experiences of those in the Bible and your experiences with God? Are there any things you read about repeatedly but have never seen personally? If so, why do you think this is true?

  2. From what you've heard of what God is presently doing overseas, have you sensed any differences between what He is doing among His people there and what He is doing where you are? If so, why do you think this is?

  3. Do you have any close friends who are charismatic or Pentecostal? If so, have you heard them describe things God is doing in their lives that have never happened to you? How do you explain the differences?

  4. A personal relationship involves regular, tangible communication between two people. How would you describe your tangible experience with God? How does it happen for you? How often does it happen?

5. Jesus promised, "You will receive power when the Holy Spirit comes on you" (Acts 1:8). As you have read this familiar promise, what have you thought and felt? In what ways have you personally experienced the power of the Holy Spirit?

CHAPTER 6: Choosing Your Wineskin

Searching the Scriptures

The Holy Spirit – Rebirth, When the Spirit Comes In

When does the Holy Spirit begin to work in our lives? When does He actually come into us to begin His empowering work? When are we "baptized *with* the Holy Spirit"? When are we "baptized *by* the Spirit" into the body of the church? What are the first changes we begin to experience when the Spirit comes in? These are good questions. Let's see what God has to say about these things.

- Jesus tells us that the Spirit begins to speak to us well before we put our faith in Him. According to John 6:43-51,60-65; 16:5-11, what does the Spirit do before we commit ourselves to Jesus? Did you experience this? If so, in what ways?

- In His well-known visit with Nicodemus, Jesus explained that to enter the kingdom of God and experience its present and future benefits, a person must be born again. In this famous conversation, Jesus described how and when the Spirit actually comes into us to give us the life of God. What does He tell us in John 3:1-21?

- First John the Baptist and later Jesus referred to our first "dousing" with the Spirit as being "baptized with the Holy Spirit." After reading Matthew 3:1-12 and Acts 1:1-5; 2:38-39, how would you explain to someone how he or she can "receive" or "be baptized with" the Holy Spirit?

- What do the following passages say about when the Spirit enters a person's life? 1 Corinthians 6:9-11; Ephesians 1:13-14; Titus 3:3-7

- Romans 8:1-17 describes not only Christ being "in" us through His Spirit but also several of the first effects we experience when newly reborn. From what Paul writes, what can we expect to experience from the Spirit after He comes into us?

- First Corinthians 12:12-13 tells us that we are not only baptized *with* the Holy Spirit but also baptized *by* the Holy Spirit into the body of Christ (that is, connected to all other believers and made part of His eternal family). From what you know about when we become part of God's family (remember John 3 and Romans 8), when would you conclude we are connected to His body?

- So when are we born again, baptized with the Holy Spirit, and baptized by one Spirit into one body? Has this happened to you? If so, what were the first clear changes you noticed in your life?

Sharing Your Life

1. As you think of the old and new wineskins in Jesus' parable, which do you tend to be most naturally? Why? What are the factors that make you either eager or reluctant for spiritual change?

2. "Tradition trumps Scripture." Have you ever seen this tendency in a church, mission, or spiritual community? How about in your personal life? If so, why do you think it happened?

3. As you think of pursuing unfamiliar but biblical experiences with God (for example, praying for the sick, hearing God's voice, or taking authority over evil spirits), what, if anything, causes you to hesitate? What barriers hold you back?

4. If the people who raised you in the faith knew that you were reading this book and considering these ideas, what would they think? How does this affect you?

5. "Just go by the book." If you just went by the Book as you understand it, is there anything you would be doing differently in your life with God? If so, what would it be?

CHAPTER 7: New Territory

Searching the Scriptures

The Holy Spirit – His Promised Power

Jesus clearly promises that the Holy Spirit will bring a dramatic, tangible surge of power to all He enters. The Greek word for the Spirit's power is *dunamis*, from which we get our word *dynamite*.

- Read Acts 1:1-9. What does this passage teach us about the Holy Spirit?

- What do the following passages teach us about the power of the Holy Spirit? Acts 1:8; Romans 15:13-19; 1 Corinthians 4:19-20; Ephesians 3:14- 21; 2 Timothy 1:7

- Specifically, what does the power of the Holy Spirit do for us? An easy way to remember the Bible's promises about the Spirit's power is to remember that He gives us R-E-S-T:

- *He Reveals.* He empowers us to *know* God and His ways (for example, His gospel, wisdom, love, and hope) and to understand, remember, and realize things we could not grasp without Him. This is a huge help to our thinking, teaching, worship, and emotions. (See John 14:26; 1 Corinthians 2:10-16; Ephesians 1:15-23; 3:14-21; 1 John 2:20-27.)

- *He Empowers.* He empowers us to *do* miracles — to do the works of Jesus; to continue the "signs and wonders" we see among the early Christians (for example, healing, casting out demons, and prophesying); to show God's compassion; to reveal the blessings of the coming kingdom; and to confirm the authority of the gospel. This is a big help both in evangelism and in relieving suffering among believers and unbelievers alike. (See John 14:12; Romans 15:17-19; 1 Corinthians 4:18-21; 12–14; 1 Thessalonians 1:5; Hebrews 2:1-4.)

- *He Speaks.* He empowers us to *hear* God personally and presently (for example, through visions, dreams, our conscience, promptings in our spirit, and prophetic words from others). This provides help in speaking to others (see Luke 12:12), finding God's direction (see Acts 13:1-3), doing right (see Romans 8:14; 9:1), and praying (see Ephesians 6:18).

- *He Transforms.* He empowers us to *change* into the image of Christ (to think, feel, and act like Jesus), to break the enslaving grip of sin, to choose righteousness over evil, and to become holy. He directs us toward right, restrains us from doing wrong, and strengthens us for good. This helps us say no to sin and yes to goodness. It also provides the power to break addictions and to replace the "hangover" of sin (the shame and anguish we feel and the damage it does to ourselves and others) with the "fruit of righteousness" (peace, honor, and joy). (See Romans 8:1-17; 15:14-16; 2 Corinthians 3:15-18; Galatians 5:16-23; Ephesians 3:14-21; 5:15-21.)

- Read the passages above and summarize what each tells us about what the power of the Spirit can do for our lives and ministries.

- What do you want the Spirit to do in your life? Why not stop right now and ask (see Luke 11:11-13)?

- In 2 Corinthians 13:14, we read about the "fellowship of the Holy Spirit," which refers to a constant, tangible relationship. In Ephesians 1:13-14, we read that the Spirit is a "deposit," or down payment, which refers to something we can experience now that assures us that future promises will be fulfilled.

- What do each of these passages teach us to expect about the present working of the Holy Spirit?

- In what ways have you experienced the fellowship and deposit of the Spirit in your life?

Sharing Your Life

1. As you have tried to help hurting people, have you ever found yourself thinking, *I wish God still did the things He did in the Bible*? If so, share your experience.

2. Have you read anything — biographies, "Spirit" books, magazine articles, newsletters — that stretched your thinking about the presence and power of God? If so, what did you read about, and how did you respond?

3. Have you everseenorexperiencedfirsthandanything that left you amazed and stretched your thinking about the power of God? If so, what? How have your thoughts about that experience developed since it happened? Reflecting back on what you've seen and heard, what would

be a good next step to responsibly learn more about the power God makes available to His people today?

CHAPTER 8: The Wall Is Coming Down!

Search the Scriptures

The Holy Spirit – His Continuous Filling

In his letters to the early believers, Paul wrote repeatedly about the Spirit's daily working in our lives through His continuous inner voice. We commonly call this the Spirit's leading or our "conscience" (Romans 9:1). This steady stream of inner prompting that gives us the ability to do good, refrain from evil, sense what's true, and pray is what Paul refers to when He tells us to be "led by the Spirit" (Romans 8:14), "live by the Spirit" (Galatians 5:16), "keep in step with the Spirit" (Galatians 5:25), and "pray in the Spirit" (Ephesians 6:18). We have all heard the Spirit's inner voice speak to us: "Go over and talk to that person. Give your sister a call. That passage of Scripture is for you right now. Don't go there. Don't say that." When we obey this familiar inner voice of the Spirit, we are being "filled with the Spirit." We are allowing the Spirit to control our thinking, our feeling, our speaking, our looking, and our walking, much like wine controls those who drink it. This is the continuous filling of the Spirit commanded in the well-known words of Ephesians 5:18 and referred to in the other passages above.

- Read what God tells us in the following passages. What are the benefits of being continuously filled with the Spirit? Romans 8:1-17; 15:13; Galatians 5:16-26; Ephesians 5:15-21

- Can you think of a time when you were filled with the Spirit? What

- happened as a result?

- Can you think of a time when you were not filled with the Spirit? What happened?

Sharing Your Life

1. In your spiritual growing up, did you ever bump into the wall of suspicion- fear-criticism that has separated Word people and Spirit people? If so, what form did that bump take?

2. What, if any, signs have you noticed that the Word-Spirit wall is coming down?

3. In what ways do you sense that distance and separation still continue between the two neighborhoods?

4. In your estimation, what can Word people learn from Spirit people and vice versa?

5. As you think about the Christian gatherings you've been part of — church, small-group fellowships, conferences, and so on — what signs do you see that there is a fresh appreciation for the ministry of the Spirit among Word people? How has this change affected you personally?

CHAPTER 9: Completing the Picture

Searching the Scriptures

The Holy Spirit – His Dramatic Filling

As you read what the Bible tells us about the Spirit's work among God's people, you will notice that He fills not only in the sense of giving continuous direction for holy living but also in the sense of providing a dramatic touch. While the continuous filling is like a steady wind filling a sail, the dramatic filling is more like a tornado hitting a barn. In the dramatic fillings we see in the Bible, there are astonishing explosions of supernatural power — at times frightening, disruptive, and confusing. Buildings shake (see Acts 4:31), people fall over and are unable to move (see 1 Samuel 19:18-24; Daniel 10:7-17; Revelation 1:9-20), some people become extraordinarily courageous (see 1 Samuel 11:6-8; Acts 4:8-20,31; 7:54- 58), others erupt into prophesying by speaking words directly from heaven (see Numbers 11:24-30; 1 Samuel 10:5-11; Luke 1:41-42,67-79), still others erupt into languages they have never learned (see Acts 2:1-13; 10:44-48; 19:1-7), one is healed of physical disease (see Acts 9:17-19), and a few go into vision-filled trances (see Ezekiel 2–3; Acts 10:9-19).

In the nineteenth century, some began to misname their dramatic fillings as "the baptism of the Spirit" (which, as you have seen, is the biblical term for the Spirit's initial coming at conversion). Others erroneously declared that such dramatic fillings were essential to empowered holiness and anointed ministry. In the twentieth century, most Pentecostals and many charismatics began to teach that these dramatic fillings were always accompanied by speaking in tongues (which is clearly not true from a simple survey of the Bible's Spirit-filling stories and its teaching on the gift of tongues).

The unfortunate result of all the misstatements and misunderstandings was that most Word people stopped thinking and talking about the Spirit's dramatic filling entirely. This rich piece of life with God was largely lost to most — along with all appreciation for the wide variety of wonderful things He does through it. This is your opportunity to recover a powerfully transforming and often-missing piece of life with God.

- Read each of the passages listed above. For each, notice the following:

- What did the Spirit do to those who were filled?

- What was the impact on the people involved?

- What did those who were filled do to get the Spirit to touch them so dramatically?

- Have you ever experienced anything like any of the stories you've read? If so, what happened, and how did it affect you?

Sharing Your Life

1. If you wanted to see a more robust ministry of the Spirit, where could you go in your area to see it done well? What would be the benefits of taking time to visit this place? What would be the risks?

2. If you wanted to hear about the power of the Spirit from someone who knows about it firsthand, whom could you talk to? How would you begin this conversation?

3. Where in your life do you need a dramatic inner breakthrough from God? Where would an answer to prayer make a big difference? Who in your area does healing prayer with some expectancy that God might answer? How do you feel about asking that group or person to pray for you?

4. What one practical step could you take to experience the present power of God? Are you willing to take it? Why or why not?

5. For one week, try the "red pen experiment" (see page 122). As you read your Bible, mark anything that expresses or describes strong emotion (for example, great joy, sorrow, amazement, affection, or devotion). Notice how God feels about feelings.

CHAPTER 10: The Purpose of Passion

Searching the Scriptures

The Holy Spirit – His Gifts

The gifts of the Spirit, or *charismata* as they are called in Greek, are supernatural abilities distributed to each believer "for the common good" (1 Corinthians 12:7). While every believer has at least one spiritual gift, there is no gift common to all (see 1 Corinthians 12:29-30, where it is expected the questions will be answered with a no). We are repeatedly told to "eagerly desire" spiritual gifts (1 Corinthians 12:31; see 14:1,39), "especially the gift of prophecy" (1 Corinthians 14:1). One of the great ironies of our day is that God specifically tells us, "Now about spiritual gifts, brothers, I do not want you to be ignorant" (1 Corinthians 12:1). Yet many Word people have deliberately avoided the subject, except for an occasional, superficial glance.

Let's take the plunge and see what the Bible has to say about this fascinating subject that is far more energizing to our life and ministry than most of us have imagined.

There are five passages that discuss spiritual gifts directly and many stories in both the Old and New Testament that illustrate them. The five passages are Romans 12:3-8; 1 Corinthians 12–14; Ephesians 4:7-16; 1 Thessalonians 5:19-22; and 1 Peter 4:10-11.

- Read these five passages in one sitting and make a list of all the gifts mentioned.

- For each spiritual gift, try to think of a biblical story that describes it being used (for example, word of knowledge— Nehemiah 8:8; word of wisdom— 1 Kings 3:16-28; prophecy—John 4:16-30).

- Beside each gift, describe the benefit you would receive if someone used it for you.

- Put an asterisk beside the gifts you have seen in practice and a double asterisk beside the ones you think you might have. If there are gifts you have never seen, why do you think that is?

- Regarding the ceasing of the gifts, where in these passages do you find the writers suggesting that some gifts might eventually pass away?

- If you read carefully, you'll notice that Paul tells us plainly that the time will come when at least some gifts will "cease" (1 Corinthians 13:8-12). According to this passage, when specifically will these gifts pass away?

Sharing Your Life

1. If you did the "red pen experiment," what did you discover?

2. When was the last time you consciously felt a deep emotion in your relationship with God? How did you express it?

3. How do you feel when other people become emotional over spiritual things in your presence? What do you appreciate? What makes you uneasy?

4. Very practically, what can you do to take a next step in biblically expressing your emotions toward other people? Toward God?

CHAPTER 11: The Value of Experience

Searching the Scriptures

The Holy Spirit – His Gifts (continued)

The most extensive instruction on the Spirit's gifts is in 1 Corinthians 12–14. To understand the ministry of the Spirit in your life and the lives of those around you, it is important to read this portion of God's Word carefully. Let's look at it section by section and think about how it might apply to us today.

- *First Corinthians 12:1-11.* Paul begins with three paragraphs about the basics of all spiritual gifts. Briefly summarize what each paragraph tells us about spiritual gifts.

Verses 1-3

Verses 4-6

Verses 7-11

- *First Corinthians 12:12-31.* Here Paul addresses two healthy and two natural but unhealthy perspectives on the obvious and dramatic differences we see among believers in the area of their spiritual gifts. Describe these four perspectives.

    - Healthy (verses 12-13)

    - Unhealthy (verses 14-20)

    - Unhealthy (verses 21-26)

    - Healthy (verses 27-31)

- *First Corinthians 13:1-13.* This is the famous "Love Chapter." Significantly, it is in the middle of God's longest discussion on how to think, *talk, and act* in the area of spiritual gifts. The point is simple: Whatever our spiritual gifts, it is vital that we use them in a way that brings good to others. Read each paragraph carefully and summarize what it tells us about exercising spiritual gifts in love.

  - Verses 1-3

  - Verses 4-7

  - Verses 8-12

  - Verse 13

- *First Corinthians 14:1-25.* Throughout the last half of this letter, Paul answers questions sent to him from the Corinthians (see 1 Corinthians 7:1). Paul continues his instruction on spiritual gifts by answering specific questions pertaining to three gifts that were evidently causing trouble in the Corinthian church (and continue to cause trouble among Christians today): tongues — the ability given by the Holy Spirit to some believers to "utter mysteries with his spirit" in an unlearned language, human or otherwise (verse 2); interpretation of tongues — the ability given by the Holy Spirit to some believers to translate the meaning of tongues (see verses 5,13,27); and prophecy — the ability given by the Holy Spirit to some believers to receive and deliver messages directly from God to a group or an individual (see verses 3,24-26). Specifically, Paul applies the law of love to these three gifts and explains how to use each well. As you read this section, answer these questions:

- What do you learn about each of these gifts and their potential benefit to us?

- How should each gift be used in love?

- *First Corinthians 14:26-40.* Here Paul delivers "the Lord's command." (verse 37) Concerning the use of these three gifts "when you come together" (verse 26).

- Summarize the specific instruction given for each gift.

- Compare the instructions given with your experience in Christian gatherings. In what ways are there similarities? How are there differences, and why do you think they exist?

- Where and how do you think these instructions should be applied today?

- *Summary.* Think back over 1 Corinthians 12–14 and list any important conclusions you have drawn from your study of this passage.

Sharing Your Life

1. We have all heard about the importance of physical touch not only for newborns but for all of us throughout our lives. What do you think about the importance of "spiritual touch"— tangible, personal experience with God?

2. At random, pick any major character in the Old Testament. Think through what you know of his or her life. What tangible experience did he or she have with God? What was the effect of these encounters on that character? Now do the same with any New Testament character. What do these two stories teach us about personal experience with God?

3. How do you feel about intentionally pursuing experience with God? What reasons would you give to encourage someone to do it? What cautions would you mention

4. How would you respond to the following questions regarding experience with God?

- When was the last time you received a clear, specific answer to prayer?

- When was the last time you saw God do something only He could have done?

- When was the last time God spoke personally to you?

CHAPTER 12: The Secret's Out

Searching the Scriptures

The Holy Spirit – How Should We Respond to Him?

As we read about the Spirit in the Bible, we find that He speaks to us in a variety of ways: through the words of the Bible (see 2 Peter 1:20-21), through the warnings of our conscience (see John 16:5-11; Romans 9:1), through the direction of His inner voice (see Isaiah 30:20-21; Romans 8:14), through His comforting assurance (see Romans 8:15-17), and through prophetic messages from others (see Acts 21:10-11). When we sense the Spirit speaking to us, how should we respond? Let's listen as God tells us what to do and what to avoid.

- *What we should do.* Each of the following passages describes a positive response to the Spirit's influence. What do you think each of these influences feels like practically? What does the positive response look like? Galatians 5:16-26; Ephesians 5:15-21; Acts 13:1-3

- *What we should avoid.* The following passages describe wrong responses to the Spirit. What do you think each means? How can you avoid these responses? Matthew 12:31-32; Acts 5:3; 7:51; Ephesians 4:30; 1 Thessalonians 5:19; Hebrews 10:29

Sharing Your Life

1. *Valuing your heritage.* In exploring new dimensions of life with God, what do you find particularly valuable from your spiritual past? How can you protect these old treasures as you continue to discover new ones?

2. *Friends' reactions.* As you have begun to explore the areas of worship and the power of the Spirit, what kinds of reactions have you received from the people around you? How have these reactions helped or hindered you?

3. *Talking about renewal.* As you have tried to talk about your new interests, thoughts, and experiences with God, what helps others to understand and think with you? What has proven counterproductive?

4. *Criticism and opposition.* Whenever we are considering change, especially spiritual change, it is natural for those around us to feel some concern. After all, the safety of our souls and the souls of those we influence are at stake. In fact, the usual response to any spiritual shift is at least some skepticism and opposition. Have you experienced this from those who know the changes going on in you? If so, how has it made you feel? How have you responded? What have you learned in the process?

5. *Practicing your new discoveries.* As you think about what God is teaching you, what seems to be the wisest way to practice what you are learning in your present ministry to others?

6. *Renewal in your church.* What, if any, attempts have been made in your church or ministry to introduce more intimate worship or more of the tangible presence of God? How have they been received? How can you continue learning new things about God in a way that most supports your present church or ministry?

7. *The need to move.* If you ever felt the need to leave your present church or ministry to continue your journey, how could you do it in a way that would best preserve your relationships with those you leave behind?

EPILOGUE. More - And Still More

Sharing Your Life

1. At present, God may be dousing you with refreshing renewal in the areas of more intimate worship and the ministry of the Spirit. Do you have any sense of other missing pieces He may want to restore to bring future renewal to your life? If so, what are they?

2. What might the impact on your life be if you took these missing pieces back?

ABOUT THE AUTHOR

Roc Bottomly graduated from the Air Force Academy in 1969 as a distinguished graduate with a BS in astronautical engineering. As a cadet, he trusted Christ through the Navigators' ministry and worked closely with the Navigators as a lay leader in military, collegiate, and community ministries throughout his service years.

After fulfilling his military commitment, Roc left his pilot wings for Dallas Theological Seminary, where he graduated with high honors and a master's degree in theology.

After being the senior pastor of two growing community churches, Roc helped plant Bridgeway Church in Oklahoma City. Bridgeway was one of the original Word-Spirit churches created to combine the strengths of the evangelical church with those of the charismatic church. From 1995 to 2001, Bridgeway grew from start-up to eight hundred members with house churches across the Oklahoma City metro area.

Following seven years as the Senior Fellow for Marriage Studies at the Focus on the Family Institute in Colorado Springs, Roc returned to Oklahoma City to be the Lead Pastor at Our Lord's Community Church, a congregation committed to making disciples who live by the truth of the Word and the power of the Spirit. In 2016, Roc became Our Lord's Pastor Emeritus.

Roc has been married to his wife, Bev, since 1974. They have four grown children and thirteen grandchildren... and you don't have to ask how they spend most of their time!

ENDNOTES

PREFACE

1. Stanley M. Burgess, ed., and Eduard M. van der Maas, assoc. ed., *The New International Dictionary of Pentecostal and Charismatic Movements* (Grand Rapids, MI: Zondervan, 2002), 286–287, table 1.

CHAPTER 3: BIG QUIESTIONS

1. *Forging Godly Servant Leaders: Dallas Theological Seminary 2000-2001 Catalogue* (Dallas: Dallas Theological Seminary, 2000), 157.

2. Charles C. Ryrie, *Basic Theology* (Wheaton, IL: Victor, 1987), 372.

CHAPTER 5: AWAKENING

1. Paul Eshleman, *The* JESUS *Film Project*, September 15, 1995.

2. Paul Eshleman, *The* JESUS *Film Project*, November 6, 1997.

3. Paul Eshleman. *The* JESUS *Film Project*, November 8, 1995.

CHAPTER 7: NEW TERRITIORY

1. John Wimber, *Power Evangelism* (San Francisco: Harper & Row, 1986), 32–33.

CHAPTER 8: THE WALL IS COMING DOWN!

1. Stanley M. Burgess, ed., and Eduard M. van der Maas, assoc. ed., *The New International Dictionary of Pentecostal and Charismatic Movements* (Grand Rapids, MI: Zondervan, 2002), 286–287, table 1.

2. Vinson Synan, *The Century of the Holy Spirit: 100 Years of Pentecostal and Charismatic Renewal, 1901-2001* (Nashville: Nelson, 2001), 2.

3. Peter Wagner, *The Third Wave of the Holy Spirit: Encountering the Power of Signs and Wonders Today* (Ann Arbor, MI: Vine Books, 1988), 16.

4. John MacArthur's book *Charismatic Chaos* (Zondervan, 1992) is a critique of the errors he saw in the charismatic movement.

5. *Microsoft Encarta Encyclopedia 99*, s. v. "Fall of Berlin Wall," (reviewed by Anna J. Merritt and Richard L. Merritt), (accessed January 5, 2005).

6. Paul Stanley (executive vice president, Navigators International Leadership Team), in discussion with the author, April 1995.

7. Doug Banister in an interview, *Zondervan Church Source*, http://www.zondervanchurchsource.com/inbanister.htm.

8. Charles R. Swindoll, *Flying Closer to the Flame* (Dallas: Word, 1993), 13–14.

9. Francis Chan, *Forgotten God: Reversing Our Tragic Neglect of the Holy Spirit* (Colorado Springs, CO: David C Cook, 2009), 15, 22.

10. Dallas Willard, *Hearing God* (Downers Grove, IL: InterVarsity Press, 1999), 9.

11. Jerry White, *Worldwide Newsletter*, no. 50, May 2004.

CHAPTER 10: THE PURPOSE OF PASSION

1. Robert E. Webber, *Blended Worship: Achieving Substance and Relevance in Worship* (Peabody, MA: Hendrickson, 1996), back cover.

2. Brad Kilman, "We Are Hungry," Brad Kilman Publishing, 1999.

3. Charlie Hall, "Salvation," Generation Music, 1997.

4. Jonathan Edwards, *Religious Affections: A Christian's Character before God* (Minneapolis: Bethany, 1996), 10–11.

CHAPTER 11: THE VALUE OF EXPERIENCE

1. James Dobson, *Bringing Up Boys* (Wheaton, IL: Tyndale, 2001), 58–59.

2. Colonel Heath Bottomly, handwritten letter, October 25, 1969.

3. Bow Bottomly, personal journal entry, June 13, 1995.

CHAPTER 12: THE SECRET'S OUT

1. Stanley M. Burgess, ed., and Eduard M. van der Maas, assoc. ed., *The New International Dictionary of Pentecostal and Charismatic Movements* (Grand Rapids, MI: Zondervan, 2002), 286–287, table 1.

CPSIA information can be obtained
at www.ICGtesting.com
Printed in the USA
LVHW081221280120
644930LV00030B/1208